Productive
TEACHING
in the Christian School

by Dr. Carl D. Herbster

Bob Jones University Press, Greenville, South Carolina 29614

Productive Teaching in the Christian School
by Carl D. Herbster

NOTE:
The fact that materials produced by other publishers are referred to in this volume does not constitute an endorsement by Bob Jones University Press of the content or theological position of materials produced by such publishers. The position of Bob Jones University Press, and the University itself, is well known. Any references and ancillary materials are listed as an aid to the student or the teacher and in an attempt to maintain the accepted academic standards of the publishing industry.

ISBN 0-89084-463-1
Printed in the United States of America

20   19   18   17   16   15   14   13   12   11   10   9   8   7   6

Acknowledgments

- To my wife, Debbie, for supporting me and allowing me the time to write this book
- To Craig Krueger for all his help in editing
- To Lynn Heusinger, Greg Woolley, Brenda Swofford, and the other Tri-City staff members for their contributions to my life and to my book
- To my secretary, Beverly Oller, and the other secretaries at Tri-City who spent hours typing manuscripts
- To all the Christian school teachers across the country who have sat in my workshops throughout the years to help me formulate the ideas which are presented in this book
- To my sons, Matthew, Mark, and Michael, for being good examples of what Christian education should produce

Dedication

This book is dedicated to all Christian school teachers. Your ministry is often taken for granted; yet you continue to serve with expertise, experience, excitement, and humility. According to the Lord's admonition: "let us not be weary in well doing: for in due season we shall reap, if we faint not" (Gal: 6:9).

Contents

Chapter 1
The Teacher Is the Key

The disciple is not above his master: but every one that is perfect shall be as his master. (Luke 6:40)

And the things that thou hast heard of me among many witnesses, the same commit thou to faithful men, who shall be able to teach others also. (II Tim. 2:2)

"Ring ring ring!"

"Hello. This is Carl Herbster."

"Yes, Dr. Herbster! This is Mr. So-and-so. I'm interested in starting a Christian school, and I was just wondering whose curriculum I should use."

"Well, Mr. So-and-so, I believe you ought to use your own curriculum."

"No, no, no, Dr. Herbster. You don't understand. What I mean is, which curriculum should I use—Bob Jones University Press? A Beka? Rod and Staff? ACE? Alpha Omega? ABC? etc., etc. Which curriculum should I use?"

"No, sir, you don't understand. Curriculum is learning experiences and course offerings that you use to accomplish the goal of Christ-likeness in your young person. It's more than books. You really should use your own curriculum. Besides, who is going to teach in your Christian school?"

"Oh, I hadn't really thought about that. I thought if I used the right curriculum, it wouldn't matter who teaches—just anybody could do it. I do have Mrs. Smith, who faithfully raised three boys. I guess if she can raise three boys, surely she can teach. And besides, she will work for nothing."

"You must get the right type of teachers—godly, qualified teachers. They will do a good job with whatever materials you choose to use in the classroom. Sir, remember, the teacher is the key."

God's Emphasis: People Or Programs?

Regrettably, this conversation is not completely fictional. In the Christian school movement, a philosophy exists that says if you have the proper textbooks it doesn't matter who teaches the material from those textbooks. Any warm body will do. ←
The emphasis has been put on books instead of on the Christ-like model, the teacher. The Bible teaches that it is impossible to get the best education for students in the Christian school unless they have the best possible model in the teacher. In Luke 6:40 the Lord Jesus Christ Himself states that the disciple is not above his master: "But every one that is perfect shall be as his master." The Scripture here indicates that students will be unlikely to excel the teacher either spiritually or academically. Whether the teacher is a pastor, a parent, or a Christian schoolteacher, the principle is the same: the teacher is the key. A person cannot teach what he does not know. Therefore, a student will not learn spiritual or academic truths from a teacher who has not learned them himself.

Some teachers believe that books alone can teach a child. Of course, students can and should learn on their own (II Tim. 2:15), but they should never be left totally to themselves (Prov. 29:15). A student left entirely to himself to grapple with the spiritual and academic questions of our day will usually become frustrated and discouraged. Independent study is necessary and helpful in developing discipline, independence, and creative thinking. However, independent study is at best a weak method of teaching students how to think, reason, and relate. Only a teacher who challenges a student to higher mental feats can accomplish this task. If a Christian school is to be effective, teacher-directed learning activities and teacher-supervised independent studies must be present. Most students are not motivated to accomplish their potential without encouragement and inspiration from a teacher.

Many studies point out the importance of the teacher in the classroom. One such study, published by the National Science Foundation in 1978, discussed the status of science, mathematics, and social studies education in the nation's elementary and secondary schools. One report, written specifically on science education, stated that within any classroom the science taught and the way it is taught depend primarily on what the individual teacher believes, knows, and does. Numerous studies indicate that the type of instruction does affect student learning. No doubt the teacher is the most important instructional variable. In the conclusion to the study, the researcher stated that teachers must assume more responsibility for creating conditions which will enhance their efforts in the classroom. This expectation may seem to be unreasonable, but teachers and administrators must find ways to allow time for unhurried thought and deliberate planning. Complete responsibility for what happens in science teaching does not rest on the shoulders of the teacher, but a successful school program that enhances education is solely dependent on what the teachers do with their students. Unmistakably, the teacher is the key.

Of course, Christian educators do not plan programs simply because of what the studies say. They plan them because the Word of God puts the emphasis on the teacher. Why else would God have given the gift of teaching to *people* in the church (Rom. 12:7; Eph. 4:11)? Why else would Paul tell the leaders (people) of the church that they must be apt to teach (I Tim. 3:2)? *People* are of utmost importance to God. A Christian school will be only as good as the *people* that make it up. In a similar way, the instruction in a Christian school will be only as good as the teachers who are doing the instructing. The teacher is the key.

The Teacher's Responsibility

Many teachers are so dependent on textbooks and teacher's manuals that often the textbooks determine what they say, when they say it, and even how long they say it. This overdependence on materials promotes laziness on the teacher's part and mediocre learning on the student's part. A textbook author might provide some guidelines and creative ideas for using his materials in the classroom; but the teacher in the classroom should not attempt to do everything exactly as the book recommends, nor should he limit his creativity to what the curriculum guide offers. No author can know everything about a student sitting in a classroom halfway across the country because every student is different. Only a dedicated, well-qualified teacher can adapt the ideas given in the teacher's manual and add to them so that all the students in the classroom can comprehend the material. The teacher must know the material, know the students, and then stimulate their thinking until they know the material. The teacher should use his own personal illustrations and strive to collect supplementary teaching materials. A teacher who uses no additional information is cheating his students.

Why would a teacher shortchange the students by limiting himself strictly to the textbook material? There are two common reasons for this problem. First, many administrators, wanting to offer the best possible education for their students, put their teachers under a mandate to follow the curriculum to the letter. They believe what some textbook salesman has told them: "Stick to the curriculum. It will do a good job. If you deviate from it, we cannot be held accountable for the results." Some Christian leaders accept this thinking and force good, qualified teachers to operate under the bondage of an over-structured curriculum outline. These well-meaning leaders are not trying to be overly dominant; they are only attempting to do what they believe is best for the organization. This type of administration, though, frustrates many well-qualified teachers to the point that they move to another Christian school or leave the Christian school movement entirely. While supervision and structure are very important for the effective operation of a Christian school, the teacher must have enough flexibility within the classroom to adapt the materials to the specific needs of the students. The teacher is the key.

The second reason that many tend to rely on an over-structured curriculum is to find an easy way out of work. To develop and adapt teaching materials to meet the various needs of students takes work. It takes work to bring in outside materials. Every class is different, and every year teachers have to change their teaching techniques slightly to meet the academic and spiritual needs of the students.

Allowing teachers room for discretionary application of the materials is not the same as allowing teachers complete freedom within the classroom. Godly, well-qualified principals must supervise and work with teachers to develop the best teaching techniques and schedule for each situation. There should be some flexibility in the structure, however, since nobody is perfect in his planning. Accomplishing the educational objectives in a particular unit may take more or less time than one expects.

The Christian school movement is no longer in its infancy. Naturally, there were many imperfections in the early days of rapid growth, but the time has come to solidify growth with maturity and to upgrade the learning process rigorously. Accomplishing this goal requires continual upgrading of the quality of the Christian school staff: hiring teachers who are qualified to teach their particular subjects and requiring present teachers to continue improving their skills. The best educational materials available will never replace godly, qualified teachers. *The teacher is the key.*

Chapter 2
The Teacher's Philosophy

Wisdom is the principal thing; therefore get wisdom: and with all thy getting get understanding. (Prov. 4:7)

I press toward the mark for the prize of the high calling of God in Christ Jesus. (Phil. 3:14)

For whom he did foreknow, he also did predestinate to be conformed to the image of his Son, that he might be the first-born among many brethren. (Rom. 8:29)

Who ever heard of a factory worker who goes to work every day not knowing what it is he is working to produce? Even the fellow that produces the widgets for the assembly line knows which whatzit his widget is for, but many—too many—Christian teachers are unable to articulate a clear answer to the question, "What is your goal in the Christian school classroom?" It seems as though many are simply trying to make it through another day or are just teaching a particular subject. Unfortunately, their ultimate goal is not clear in their minds.

Priorities

There are four principal priorities in the operation of a Christian school: philosophy, people, program, and plant.

The physical *plant* is the least important feature of the Christian school. However, there is no excuse for buildings and grounds that are unkempt. Even if buildings are not the newest and most modern, even if the grounds are not the most spacious, they should be neat and clean.

The *program* of the Christian school is the set of day-to-day procedures that facilitate teaching and learning. The program includes such things as curriculum, textbooks, scheduling, and finances. Every school is unique, and its program must be tailor-made to the school's specific ministry, considering the area of the country, the type of students, and other situations found in the community. Furthermore, every Christian school should be continuously evaluating its program and making adjustments to enhance quality Christian education.

People are the key to the Christian school movement. Those operating a Christian school must realize that their school will be only as good as the people they hire. These people must have a philosophy in harmony with the leadership of the school; and they must have an expertise in the grades or subject areas assigned to them. People are the greatest asset to any ministry. Quality organizations depend on quality people.

Everybody in the Christian school (people) and everything that takes place in the Christian school (program) must revolve around one common Biblical philosophy. To serve effectively in a Christian school, a teacher must understand the Biblical philosophy of Christian education as well as believe and practice it.

The word *philosophy* comes from Greek words meaning "love of wisdom." Since the garden of Eden, man has wanted to be wise and has striven to know all truth (Gen. 3:5). In searching for the truth, each man develops a system of values and beliefs that guide his every action. This system is his philosophy of life. Many, however, cannot articulate their philosophy, although they act upon it.

The Christian must develop his philosophy by studying God's truth, the Bible (John 17:17). The Apostle Paul warns us not to be spoiled by the philosophies of this world—philosophies such as situation ethics, humanism, and materialism (Col. 2:8). He defines a Christian philosophy as one that follows after Christ and not after the world because in Christ "are hid all the treasures of wisdom and knowledge" (Col. 2:3). The Christian's philosophy must be based on the Lord Jesus Christ as He is revealed in the Scripture. A man who derives his system of values and beliefs from any source other than God's Word is susceptible to worldly influences and error.

The Purpose Of Christian Education

Although the Bible does not mention the Christian school, it says much about the education of young people. God makes plain that His goal for all Christians is that they "be perfect, throughly furnished unto all good works" (II Tim. 3:17). To accomplish this task, God gives men various gifts "for the perfecting of the saints, for the work of the ministry, for the edifying of the body of Christ: till we all come in the unity of the faith, and of the knowledge of the Son of God, unto a perfect man, unto the measure of the stature of the fullness of Christ" (Eph. 4:12-13). These verses describe the goal of Christian education: to create in every young person the likeness of Christ. Christian education should develop Christians whose activities in this life anticipate their eventual conformity to the image of Christ (Rom. 8:29).

The Responsibility For Christian Education

Christian education should take place first in the Christian home. In the Old Testament, parents are commanded to "teach [God's Word] diligently unto [their] children" (Deut. 6:7). In the New Testament they are commanded to "bring them up in the nurture and admonition of the Lord" (Eph. 6:4). These commands are directed to Christian parents, who bear the ultimate responsibility for the success or failure of their children's education.

Another institution with God-given responsiblities for education is the church. In the Great Commission Jesus tells His church—all Christians—to go and "teach all nations, baptizing them in the name of the Father, and of the Son, and of the Holy Ghost: teaching them to observe all things whatsoever I have commanded you" (Matt. 28:19-20). Notice the order in which the Great Commission was given. The first command is to make disciples. A prerequisite to discipling is evangelism: a person must be won to Christ before he can be discipled. The second command is to baptize these converts, and the third is to teach them everything that God has commanded. Christians are to win the lost to Christ and then teach them.

In our generation the Christian school has been established as an arm of the home and, usually, of the church. It has accepted responsibility for reinforcing the Biblical teachings of the home and church. It operates *in loco parentis* (in the place of the parents). The Christian school does not relieve parents of the ultimate responsibility for the education of their children. However, its goal should be the goal of Christian parents: making the student more Christ-like.

Why Have A Christian School?

In the United States compulsory education laws require all educable children to attend school. Since Christian citizens are to "be subject unto the higher powers" (Rom. 13:1), Christian parents must make sure that their children go to school during the appropriate years for the required number of days. The government has established public schools to help parents fulfill this attendance requirement; however, public schools operate under a philosophy which is not in harmony with God's Word. Their goal is to make students worldly—to make them conform to the mores of society—a goal that completely contradicts God's goal. Scripture commands, "Be not conformed to this world: but be ye transformed by the renewing of your mind" (Rom. 12:2). As the goals of secular schools have become increasingly contrary to the goals of Christian education, new schools that meet the requirements of the attendance laws and that also allow parents to conform their children to the image of Christ have become necessary.

The reason for the Christian school is not solely to get students away from drug abuse, poor academics, poor discipline, or racial strife. The Christian school has been established to allow parents to obey God's command to give their children a Christian education and, at the same time, to obey the law of the land. No matter how the secular schools may improve academically, Christian parents must continue to turn to the Christian school to obtain Christian education since the goal of secular education is contrary to the will of God.

It is important to understand that Christian education and the Christian school are not the same. Christian education is the process of conforming the student to the image of Christ. The Christian school is a place designed to give students a large part of their Christian education. Christian education begins at salvation and continues until death. Most Christian day schools begin at kindergarten and stop at the twelfth grade.

Many people falsely assume that once a child is in a Christian school he will automatically obtain a Christian education. But many schools that are called "Christian" do not produce students that are conformed to the image of Christ. A school that is not accomplishing the goal of Christian education with a majority of its students is not truly a Christian school. On the other hand, it is possible for a child to obtain a Christian education without ever attending a Christian school. In many cases the children of missionaries and evangelists never attend a Christian school, yet they conform to the image of the Lord Jesus Christ through the training they receive at home. These Christian workers' children obtain a Christian education without the benefit of a Christian school. Since attending a Christian school does not guarantee a Christian education, and since a Christian education does not require a Christian school, the two terms are not synonymous and should not be used interchangeably.

The chart on the following page presents the problem faced by Christian schools in America. Everything within the circle labeled "Christian education" represents Christian education taking place in the lives of young people. Everything in the circle labeled "Christian school" represents the students attending a Christian school. The first rectangle, where the two circles never meet, represents a Christian school with no Christian education taking place. Students may get an academic education, but they are not being conformed to the image of Christ. The circles in the second rectangle intersect so that twenty-five percent of the young people in the Christian school are obtaining a Christian education. However, seventy-five percent failure is never satisfactory. The next rectangle represents a school with fifty percent of its students being conformed to the image of Christ. Still we should not be satisfied. Although the leaders of the Christian school realize that not one hundred percent of the students will conform to the image of Christ, they should not be content with anything less (Col. 1:28). They should continue to work toward this goal just as they should work toward the goal of becoming perfect (Matt. 5:48).

Figure 2.1

CHRISTIAN
EDUCA-
TION

A PROCESS

CHRISTIAN
SCHOOL

A PLACE

NO CHRISTIAN EDUCATION TAKING PLACE
IN CHRISTIAN SCHOOL

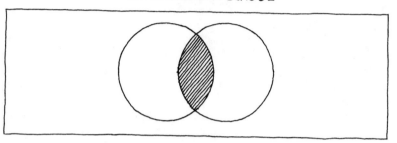

25% BEING CONFORMED TO CHRIST

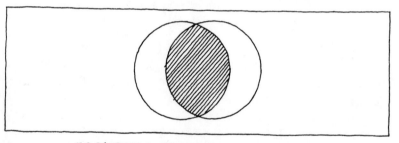

50% BEING CONFORMED TO CHRIST

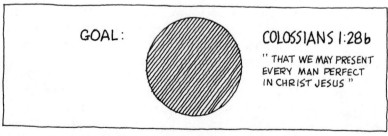

GOAL:

COLOSSIANS 1:28b

" THAT WE MAY PRESENT
EVERY MAN PERFECT
IN CHRIST JESUS "

100% BEING CONFORMED TO CHRIST

The Recipient Of Christian Education

Christian education, properly considered, is for Christians. "As education in general begins with physical birth, Christian education properly begins with spiritual rebirth" (*The Christian Philosophy of Education,* p. 4). The unsaved person cannot be conformed to the image of Christ because "the natural man receiveth not the things of the Spirit of God: for they are foolishness unto him: neither can he know them, because they are spiritually discerned" (I Cor. 2:14). The unregenerate person cannot be expected to conform his life to Christ's commandments since he does not have the Holy Spirit to teach him all truth (John 14:26; 16:13). Without the Teacher, there can be no education.

To say that Christian education is only for Christians is not to say that the Christian school is only for Christian young people. The Christian school is designed to help Christian parents, usually members of local fundamentalist churches, train young people for the Lord. Many of the children from these homes, especially those in elementary school, may not yet have come to salvation. Very probably, some of the junior and senior high students who profess to be saved really are not. For this reason, it is very important that the Christian school give clear Biblical teaching on salvation so that these young people can become "wise unto salvation through faith which is in Christ Jesus" (II Tim 3:15). Evangelism will take place in the Christian school. However, the school should not be designed primarily for evangelism; it should be designed for the education of Christians. Unless the student body of a school is predominantly Christian, the school cannot be considered a Christian school.

Recruiting Students

The best way to maintain a predominantly Christian student body is to have restrictive admissions policies. The Christian school should limit enrollment primarily to Christian young people or to those from Christian homes. Since the Christian school is designed for Christian young people, the majority of students should be recruited from fundamentalist churches in the area. Parents who want their children to develop Christ-like character should be encouraged to enroll their children. However, unsaved parents of unsaved young people should not be similarly encouraged unless they truly desire that their children be saved and conformed to the image of Christ. Many unsaved parents desire only the high academic standards and discipline that the Christian school offers, not the training in godliness that the school exists to provide.

Selecting Personnel

All people involved in a Christian school ministry must have high spiritual and academic qualifications. Every staff member must be a born-again Christian whose life evidences the fruit of the Spirit (Gal. 5:22-23) and testifies to the students of the grace of God. No matter what the position—be it teacher, coach, bus driver, or janitor—every person involved in the Christian school must first of all have a living relationship with the Lord Jesus Christ. The teaching staff must be prepared academically as well since the faculty determines the quality of the education offered (Luke 6:40). Because teachers wield a powerful influence, their spiritual and academic qualifications cannot and should not be minimized. A Christian school will never be any better than its people.

Beyond these qualifications it is especially important that each employee have a servant's heart (Matt. 20:27) and that each be willing to give of himself rather than be concerned about what he will receive for himself. This attribute is not easily acquired. It is easier to educate a teacher to be effective in the classroom than to help him cultivate a servant's heart.

Teaching and Learning

The teaching in a Christian school should prepare students to function in the activities of life and to pursue further academic training—in most cases, college. As Dr. Bob Jones, Sr., said, we must teach students "not only how to make a living but also how to live." Each subject should be presented from a Biblical point of view and made applicable to the student's Christian life, developing in him Christ-likeness.

The Christian school must teach every subject in a way that helps students to learn principles that they can apply in life's situations, forcing them to think and not merely to memorize. Students who learn only facts and not applications are not developing Biblical wisdom. Wisdom, the ability to use facts, is what God wants us to seek (Prov. 4:5-7). In order to educate young people properly, administrators and teachers must teach students to apply to everyday situations the truths that they learn.

Behavioral Standards

The Christian school should have behavioral standards consistent with Biblical principles and designed to help young people develop Christ-likeness. An important principle applicable to Christian schools is that God wants young people to possess self-control, which is developed during the application of external control (Prov. 3:11-12; Heb. 12:11). Students should expect not only to behave themselves in an orderly and controlled fashion but also to incur disciplinary measures when they do not live up to the standards set by the school. Those who consistently violate the behavioral standards of the school must be expelled so that they do not negatively influence the rest of the student body (I Cor. 5:7).

Every standard of conduct set up by the Christian school should have a Biblical basis. Though there may not be an explicit command in Scripture for every standard of behavior, the school administrator should be able to justify each standard as an application of a Biblical principle (e.g., respect for property, Luke 16:10-12; respect for authority, Rom. 13:1-7; abstinence from the appearance of evil, I Thess. 5:22). Students should be taught Biblical principles as well as the standards of behavior so that they can learn to live by principles, not just rules.

Academic Standards

The primary goal of Christian education is spirituality or Christ-likeness. However, to be Christ-like a student must "[increase] in wisdom and stature, and in favor with God and man" (Luke 2:52). The student is not progressing properly unless he is developing academically, physically, spiritually, and socially. Children can be trained spiritually, physically, and socially in the home or local church, but it is very difficult for the local church to give proper academic preparation. Personnel trained in various academic areas are not usually teaching academic subject matter in the church, nor are most parents equipped to teach every academic subject. Therefore, the Christian school is the only institution that can teach the academic material necessary for young people in the twentieth century. The Christian school should not neglect spiritual, physical, and social development, but it must stress academics since they will probably not be fully developed anywhere else.

Figure 2.2

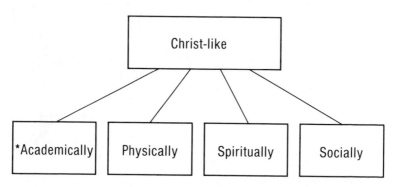

Proof of the effectiveness of a Christian school is demonstrated in the lives of the students (the product). If students do not leave a school with a burning love for the Lord Jesus Christ and with a desire to serve Him, that school has failed. The students need not be spiritual giants; however, they should at least be faithful in a good Bible-preaching church and should continue to grow spiritually. Many will go on to Christian colleges. Schools which are not producing this consistent product must re-evaluate and make positive changes in accord with the Biblical philosophy of education.

In order for a Christian school to operate effectively and efficiently, each teacher must have the same practical, Biblical philosophy of Christian education: "Can two walk together, except they be agreed?" (Amos 3:3). For the school program to work, all teachers must aim for the same Biblical goal—Christ-likeness. If a school is established or operated apart from this solid Biblical philosophy, it will not produce a Christ-like young person and therefore should not be called a Christian school.

A Biblical philosophy of Christian education must be the first priority in every Christian school. The teacher is the key in making sure that this philosophy is carried out in the classroom. Therefore, the effective Christian school teacher *must* know, understand, and practice this Biblical philosophy.

Chapter 3
The Teacher's Characteristics

Ye are our epistle written in our hearts, known and read of all men. (II Cor. 3:2)

The disciple is not above his master: but every one that is perfect shall be as his master. (Luke 6:40)

II Corinthians 3:2 might be paraphrased this way:

Your walk talks,
And your talk talks,
But your walk talks
Louder than your talk talks.

The weight of a teacher's living example far exceeds the weight of all his words. Academic competency is of great importance for a Christian teacher, but spiritual competency is even more important. The truth of Luke 6:40, that the student completing his training will tend to be like his teacher, extends beyond academics. That truth extends even to the level of students' imitating habits of dress and speech, mannerisms, and even values and philosophy that neither the teacher nor the student has directly addressed. The disciple becomes as his master—for better or for worse. What a responsibility falls upon the effective Christian teacher to be a model of Christ-likeness.

A Spiritual Christian

Brethren, if a man be overtaken in a fault, ye which are spiritual, restore such an one in the spirit of meekness; considering thyself, lest thou also be tempted. (Gal. 6:1)

The Christian school teacher is in the restoration business. Often, students are from very difficult home situations in which parents are not entirely supportive of the school's direction. Sometimes, even those homes that should be model homes— those of the faithful church members or church leaders—are shocking disappointments. The teacher is not dealing with those that are spiritually mature; he is dealing with young people. Many times, especially in the lower grades, students do not yet have the indwelling Christ of salvation; even later they are still young Christians. The teacher must be an example of what they are to be someday. In Galatians 5:22-23 God lists some of the characteristics that are important.

Love

The teacher should love students, and he should love teaching. If he does not, teaching is not the job for him. *Loving* does not mean liking everything that students do; it means having a strong desire to meet their needs even when they are "unlovely." A teacher loves his ministry and his students so much that problems and pressures do not keep him from trying to do a better job and to help students grow.

Joy

The teacher needs to let the joy in his heart be seen by his actions and attitudes. Although the teacher may approach many days with the prayer, "Lord, get me through this day," if he does not experience an overall joy in teaching, and if he does not eagerly anticipate the opportunities of teaching, then he needs to determine whether he is in the will of God.

Peace

A spiritual person does not become flustered when things— or people—go wrong. Boys and girls from chaotic homes need the influence of a teacher who manifests the peace that passes all understanding. The teacher who possesses this peace has a special ministry.

Longsuffering

It is natural to want results "yesterday," but it is supernatural to be patient with students. They do not get all of their wiggles out in the first week of school. They do not become self-actualizing, inspired scholars in the first month of school. God is not finished with them yet, and we need to keep working patiently with Him. A junior high student is not a finished product. God has not even finished shaping the lives of seniors yet—nor has He finished with the teacher. When the teacher reflects on the many imperfections in his own life, he will be inspired to be more patient toward those with whom he works.

Gentleness

Students can be very unkind, even cruel. The student who is unkind to his teacher or fellow-students needs to reap the consequences of his actions, but he needs also to see the example of gentleness in the teacher's punishment. Gentleness is the velvet glove on the iron hand. It handles each student in terms of his emotional needs. Godly gentleness helps the teacher to be firm when necessary and yet not to crush the student who is already hurting.

Goodness

Goodness manifests itself in actions that reach out to meet needs in the lives of students, parents, coworkers, and others. It is a dress for a girl with a financial need or a smile to the sad and lonely student. It is a note of congratulations to the student who has achieved some victory, small or great. Goodness is simply love in action.

A Called Servant

Whosoever will be chief among you, let him be your servant. (Matt. 20:27)

Jesus Himself came not to be served, but to serve and to give His life for others. An example of this service was the foot washing in the upper room. He wrapped Himself in a servant's towel and did the lowly task without being asked. Then He instructed those that would follow Him to do likewise.

Rather than asking "What do I *get* in pay? What do I *get* in benefits? When do I *get* a free period?", a teacher coming to a position ought to ask "What can I give? How can I become involved in the church? How can I meet the needs of others?"

A person can take classes to learn how to be a teacher, but he needs the Holy Spirit to teach him through the Word of God how to be a servant. A servant cares about the well-being of others. He sees—even seeks—needs and is satisfied in simply meeting those needs. He does not need the praise of men, but he has a hungering and thirsting to do the will of God and to serve as Christ served—in lowliness, meekness, and love.

A Student of God's Word

Study to shew thyself approved unto God, a workman that needeth not to be ashamed, rightly dividing the word of truth. (II Tim. 2:15)

Christian educators deal with young people continually. Teachers have an extraordinary need to be stable and well-grounded in the Word of God. A teacher must be able to present, clearly and simply, the plan of salvation *with the Scriptures memorized.* Next, the teacher needs to be growing daily in his own relationship with Christ by Bible reading, study, memorization, and meditation. Most schools have children from a variety of backgrounds, and all schools have children who will be seeking someone who can give a reasonable, Biblical answer for his stand on such matters as tongues, eternal security, and other doctrinal issues. The teacher must know what he believes and why he believes it. Whether in the private time one spends with God and His Word or in formal Bible training, the Christian teacher should be growing in the Scriptures.

A Faithful Church Member

Not forsaking the assembling of ourselves together, as the manner of some is; but exhorting one another: and so much the more, as ye see the day approaching. (Heb. 10:25)

Two marks of the indwelling Spirit are a love of God's Word and a love for God's people. The Christian educator should be faithful to and involved in a local church. Church attendance, however, should be assumed as part of the Christian life and leadership and as the most natural behavior for the Christian educator. It is right to have a statement of church attendance in the policies of the school, but it is wrong for the educator to go to church only because attendance is required.

A Loyal Employee

Obey them that have the rule over you, and submit yourselves: for they watch for your souls, as they that must give account, that they may do it with joy, and not with grief: for that is unprofitable for you. (Heb. 13:17)

Loyalty to an employer means that a teacher will seek the good of his administrator, even when problems arise. Loyalty is also seen in seeking to resolve problems. If some inconvenience or offense is truly insignificant, it is a sign of greatness of heart to let it go unnoticed. The greater one's heart is, the greater the personal offense which one can ignore. However, when the problem is a matter of principle dealing with the application of God's Word or is such a burr under the saddle that it hinders one's ministry, loyalty requires that one bring the problem into the open. It is Scriptural and sensible to go to the person who is responsible for the problem. If necessary, the teacher may need to take a problem to the administrator or pastor *after* a sincere attempt to resolve it at a lower level. It is not wise to hold these matters inside oneself. Loyalty seeks to believe the good and to resolve the bad.

The teacher manifests loyalty by enforcing school policy. One does not have to agree with every fine point of policy, but one must support and enforce the school's policy. If a teacher is part of an organization, it is not "their policy," but "our policy," and it is incumbent upon each staff member to present each policy in its most positive light.

A Cooperative Co-laborer

For we are labourers together with God: ye are God's husbandry, ye are God's building. (I Cor. 3:9)

The teacher is first of all a co-laborer with Christ, but not with Christ alone. The ministry of any church or school involves all of the people and their interactions with one another and with Christ.

A Christian school is a triad. It involves the Christian home, the foundation of power and authority in shaping children; the Bible-believing church, the spiritual support for the home; and finally the school, the educational part of the relationship between church and home. Teachers should be actively seeking to inform and involve the parents in the process of education, discipline, and training. The school or teacher cannot afford the reputation of trying to exclude the parents nor of being partial to some. They must involve all the parents, recognizing that it is the parents who are ultimately responsible for their children's education.

A Qualified Educator

And the things that thou hast heard of me among many witnesses, the same commit thou to faithful men, who shall be able to teach others also. (II Tim. 2:2)

Timothy was to teach others the things that he had learned from Paul. In the academic as well as the spiritual, we are to do the same; but the teacher cannot teach what he does not know. There are two reasons for desiring to have college graduates as teachers. One is credibility, and the other is that a teacher who has spent four years in college should graduate knowing something. He should know how to do more than add if he is a math major! He does not need to learn everything about classroom management, but he should come to the school with some foundation.

Sometimes an experienced teacher does not have a degree, but he should seek to get a degree from a recognized, respected school. If, however, a teacher does not have much teaching experience, he should take whatever time is required to get the *training* he needs along with the degree.

Growth does not end with a diploma. A dedicated educator will be constantly growing. He will read books, as well as educational journals, about his field and about the process of education. He will take graduate courses. Even without the objective of gaining an advanced degree, summer courses can be immensely stimulating. For some teachers, this intellectual and spiritual stimulation may be just what is needed to stave off boredom, revitalize their ministries, and keep them in Christian education.

A Loving Disciplinarian

For whom the Lord loveth he chasteneth, and scourgeth every son whom he receiveth. (Heb. 12:6)

Discipline is actually discipling, and the motive of discipline is love. True love cannot exist without discipline, and true discipline is always done in love. Either without the other is self-defeating. A teacher must start the year with the establishment of proper classroom order as a top priority. First-year teachers in particular must establish themselves early.

Discipline will sometimes require negative reinforcement, punishment, and corrective words. After a student has been disciplined, he tends to avoid the authority who disciplined him. He then needs some positive reinforcement. It may be praise for something done right or just a smile and a word of greeting in the hall. Even that is enough to let him know that the problem is past and is no longer an issue with the teacher. A spiritual teacher is kind, and he wisely interweaves the positive and the negative aspects of discipline.

A Well-groomed Testimony

For the Lord seeth not as man seeth; for man looketh on the outward appearance, but the Lord looketh on the heart. (I Sam. 16:7)

God said these words to Samuel when the prophet was seeking the right man to anoint as king. In the context, the emphasis is that God sees the heart. However, the other side of the statement sometimes is lost: man *does* look on the outward appearance. By what do men judge others? They cannot see the heart. An outward appearance that communicates a respect for God and for self, as well as a confidence that expresses itself in preparation and order must be evident. In this world where men's sinful hearts are looking for ways to reject God and His principles, "little things" like deodorant, well-groomed hair, and neat, clean clothing can make a difference. Many major corporations require their salesmen to wear dark suits and short haircuts as a means of commanding respect and projecting an image of authority. As servants of the Lord, certainly we should be as careful with our appearance and testimony.

On the other hand, the conservative Christian must not project the image of being proud and pompous. Having hair on or off the ears does not make a man more or less spiritual. It is more important that a Christian be willing to change for the sake of effective ministering. Some people will always misunderstand, assuming that any standard of dress comes from a legalistic mindset. It is the Christian educator's responsibility to have his heart right before God, who sees the heart, and to be a well-groomed testimony before men, who see the outward appearance.

A Miracle Worker

> *Verily, verily, I say unto you, He that believeth on me, the works that I do shall he do also; and greater works than these shall he do; because I go unto my Father. (John 14:12)*

What did Christ mean by "greater works"? *He* gave sight to the blind; *He* made the lame to walk; *He* stilled the raging waves on Galilee—what can the Christian teacher do? Is it not in the basic job description of the Christian school teacher to give light to young people who are spiritually blind, to teach the Christian walk to children whose walk is not right, and to still the troubled waters in young hearts? Truly, the Christian educator, co-laboring with Christ, is a miracle worker. A spiritual teacher is a direct gift of God to the Christian school. Without the right teachers, there would be no Christian education nor the miracles that happen in the Christian school year by year.

"Your walk talks, and your talk talks; but your walk talks louder than your talk talks." The ten qualifications discussed are foundational to all that follows in this book about being an effective Christian teacher.

Chapter 4
The Teacher Laboring with Others

Now he that planteth and he that watereth are one: and every man shall receive his own reward according to his own labour. For we are labourers together with God: ye are God's husbandry, ye are God's building. (I Cor. 3:8-9)

We are laborers together with God. That principle is the key factor in considering the teacher's role within the church and within the school organization. The teachers, administration, and staff are not merely "labourers together"; they are "labourers together with God." If God is not in the midst of the work, nothing good and enduring will be accomplished. We are God's building; and "except the Lord build the house, they labour in vain that build it" (Ps. 127:1). It is God's school; and unless the Lord blesses it, they labor in vain that teach there.

What does an organization of professionals need in order to labor harmoniously with each other and with God? What makes a school pleasing to the Lord and productive in His work? Effective Christian teaching requires that all staff members have a common *purpose,* understand their *places* in the organization, and practice basic *principles* of courtesy.

The Purpose of Your Calling

Every organization must have one goal. In football, the goal is to get the ball across a line. Picture this scene: On a crisp autumn day late in a football game, the score is seventeen to seventeen, and the quarterback calls a huddle. He says, "Twenty-three blue on three! Break!" But one lineman winks at his buddy and says, "Watch this. I've got my own plan." The ball is snapped, and that lineman, instead of blocking, lunges for the ball. He snatches it from his quarterback and, with his teammates pursuing him, starts running for the wrong goal line. What a mess! The whole game ends in chaos because that lineman did not have the same goal as his quarterback.

The staff members of a Christian school often do not have a common goal. As a result, the play bogs down in chaos, and many passes are fumbled or, even worse, intercepted by the opposition.

Any statement of the goal of Christian education must contain this basic idea: the goal is to see students conformed to the image of the Lord Jesus Christ (Rom. 8:29). Once the goal is understood, it will shape the direction of the curriculum, the choice of books, the handling of discipline, and the offering of extracurricular activities. All the activities of teaching and administration revolve around the accomplishment of that goal, and any activity that is not directed toward that goal is discarded or modified. No pet activity is spared; no preferred tradition is held sacred. Everything must be measured against the invariable standard: Will this help me to direct these students to be conformed to Christ's image?

It is easy to become excited about the quality academics of the Christian school. It may be easy to promote outstanding achievement test scores to the community, but if the student is a failure spiritually, then the school has failed. Unity of purpose is essential. If some teachers unduly emphasize academics or sports or if the administrator does not have the ultimate goal of conforming students to the image of Christ, confusion and conflict will come. "Can two walk together, except they be agreed?" (Amos 3:3).

A pastor may want to use his school to evangelize the community, opening it to anybody who wants private education. He intends to preach the gospel, and he hopes that some will be saved, but the teachers and administration have to work day by day with the cancerous spread of bad attitudes and spiritual coldness. They see the problems as "a little leaven [that] leaveneth the whole lump" (Gal. 5:9). When a significant percentage of students in the school are unsaved, it rapidly loses its spiritual effectiveness because "the natural man receiveth not the things of the Spirit of God: for they are foolishness unto him: neither can he know them, because they are spiritually discerned" (I Cor. 2:14).

Academics and evangelism should not be the *primary* focuses of a Christian school. Good academics and evangelism have their place in the Christian school; but to set up either of these as the primary goal while still desiring Christ-like students is double-mindedness (James 1:8), spiritual schizophrenia. To avoid this danger, the pastor, administration, and teachers of a school should search the Scriptures and together formulate a written statement of philosophy. Some foolishly assume that every well-meaning Christian teacher automatically understands the primary goal of Christian education. One primary goal should be stated—conformity to the image of Christ (Rom. 8:29)—and procedures to achieve it should be clearly delineated.

The Place in the Organization

Each member of the team must know not only the purpose of the organization but also his place in the organization. Unfortunately, roles and responsibilities in the Christian school are often vague. Few Christian schools have organizational charts or written job descriptions although these are basic in secular organizations where no higher goal than profit is sought. "The children of this world are in their generation wiser than the children of light" (Luke 16:8). A simple way to generate job descriptions in a school is to have each faculty or staff member write his own. The administrator can then review and modify the descriptions to promote efficiency and to prevent overlap and confusion. A job description is helpful to each individual, as well as to the organization, in understanding exactly what each person is expected to do and to whom he is to report.

I Corinthians 12 addresses this laboring in harmony:

For by one Spirit are we all baptized into one body. . . . For the body is not one member, but many. If the foot shall say, Because I am not the hand, I am not of the body; is it therefore not of the body? And if the ear shall say, Because I am not the eye, I am not of the body; is it therefore not of the body? If the whole body were an eye, where were the hearing? If the whole were hearing, where were the smelling? But now hath God set the members every one of them in the body, as it hath pleased him. (I Cor. 12:13-18)

The hands may get all the glory, but the feet carry the body faithfully. Elementary teachers are probably the feet in the Christian school. They have the same group all day without much of a break. However, a divinely called elementary teacher who is in God's will loves his job! The same teacher might be appalled at the suggestion of teaching English in senior high. "What? Me? Walk into that room full of boys daring *me* to teach *them* English? No way!"

The principle is this: not only has "God set the members every one of them in the body, as it hath pleased him" (I Cor. 12:18), but God also assures us that His assignment will be pleasing to us. Romans 12:2 states that God's will is *good* (for us) and *perfect* (perfectly suited to us) and *acceptable* (to us).

Many people think it would be great to be the administrator. "Boy, if I were the administrator, I know how I would straighten this place out!" Who takes the pressure when the angry parents come in? Who stands behind his teachers when the criticism comes? Who ultimately has to get the job done even when some team members fail to pull their own weight? Administration has problems to match its privileges, and the higher one goes in the chain of command, the stricter the accountability (James 3:1; cf. Num. 20:11-12).

Every faculty or staff member should know his place, faithfully perform his function, and not make decisions where he has no authority. Consider a seemingly simple situation. A student approaches a teacher and asks permission to go home. If the student is hurt or becomes the victim of a kidnaping, the teacher bears the responsibility because it was not his position to decide to let the student leave. Consequently, most schools do not allow a teacher the responsibility to grant permission to leave.

A teacher who does not believe that the school is effectively working toward the proper goal can exercise his right and responsibility to do something about it. First, of course, he should pray. Then he should approach the administrator, present the problem, and offer to be a part of the solution. If his suggestion is well received, good. If not, he has two options. In the case of a minor issue, the teacher graciously submits. In the case of a major issue, the teacher may decide that God is directing him to serve elsewhere. Never should a staff member remain and cause discord. God cannot bless the school or the individual in that situation: Christian educators must labor together in harmony.

There is joy in accomplishment, but before one can know that he has accomplished what he is expected to do, he first must know exactly what is expected of him. He must know his place in the organization.

> Honor and shame from no condition rise;
> Act well your part, there all the honor lies.
>
> Alexander Pope

Principles of Courtesy

A person can be a walking encyclopedia of educational philosophy, capable of producing from memory an organizational chart more complex than the printed circuits in a computer; but if he does not practice basic principles of Christian courtesy, he will be displeasing the Lord and his co-workers, and he will be unhappy with himself. These principles are not limited to the Christian school. They are fundamental to happy, successful relationships with people in any situation.

1. Never belittle a co-laborer publicly or privately.

Bad habits and irritating tendencies become amazingly obvious to the co-workers who labor together day by day. Criticisms can be leveled at fellow workers. There is a difference between friendly teasing and sarcastic barbs, and the boundaries of good humor will vary with every twofold relationship. Let love and discretion rule in each relationship.

Sometimes an administrator will walk into a class session and correct the teacher. This behavior is not decisive leadership; it is inconsiderate boorishness. Even if the teacher needs to correct a problem with his class, the administrator should instruct him privately and let the teacher mend his own fences.

2. Never play favorites.

Very naturally some people will be closer friends than others. That friendship is not a problem. Perhaps the ties are similarities of personalities, common interests, or a shared ministry in the church. Two single people need companionship. The fact that some people will always be closer friends than others should not produce a bias in our dealings. Be careful not to let all the praise or the preferred assignments go to those who happen to be the closest personally. Consider the needs of each person as a child of God, precious and beloved in His sight.

3. Never intentionally show up a colleague.

Good teachers tend to be competitive, and they want to do the best possible job. These are positive qualities. When the principal or another visitor is in the classroom, good teachers want everything to be at its best. Those beautiful bulletin boards—are they so painfully wrought to please the Lord and to serve Him, or are they displays of egotism? Some competition is acceptable, but too much can engage the work force in open combat. It is not the product but the motive that is in question. Do not diminish the product but alter the motives, perhaps turning some of that drive toward helping others to succeed.

A certain teacher might be so pleased with his knack for discipline that he takes it upon himself to correct students in front of their supervising teacher, usurping the other teacher's authority. Such action implies, "You can't handle your class; so I'll handle it for you." Let that never be. A Spirit-filled Christian teacher will seek to build up his co-laborers in their own estimation and in the estimation of others.

4. Never fail to give your co-laborer your undivided attention.

Common courtesy demands giving full attention to others, looking them in the eye, and giving them time to discuss their concerns. A fully attentive listener shows that he cares and that he thinks others are important. The formula for giving full attention is to "stop, look, and listen" as though the speaker were the only person in the world at that moment.

5. Always be sensitive about small things.

This principle needs to be addressed to the men—particularly to men who are administrators. Look for the little things others have done that should be commended. Look for the little problems that need correction. Ladies are more naturally attuned to those things. If a man is an administrator, he would be wise to ask a lady to check the school building just before each new year begins. He may not notice the cobwebs, the dust on the shelves, or the dead flies on the window sills, but she will.

We can call in help to maintain our buildings, but each Christian must tend to his own relationships with others. In relationships especially, little offenses and little irritations will slowly strangle healthy communication. Small discourtesies and thoughtless words are the seeds of bitterness and strife. Always be sensitive about small things.

It is "the little foxes, that spoil the vines" (Song of Sol. 2:15). Little foxes such as unanswered notes, forgotten promises, or unmet needs may seem small. Being sensitive about small matters is a big part of maintaining staff harmony.

6. Always be willing to learn from others.

> *As an earring of gold, and an ornament of fine gold, so is a wise reprover upon an obedient ear. (Prov. 25:12)*

Proverbs is replete with verses on the wisdom of accepting counsel, even in the form of rebuke. A teacher or administrator should not take it as a personal affront when someone speaks to him about a problem. Having a teachable spirit requires humility, but God pours out His grace on the humble, and He resists the proud (James 4:6).

7. Always care about your co-laborers.

Christian educators should go out of their way to help each other, not only at school but also outside school. Whether a person is having troubles with his health or his children or is just painting his house, a godly friend is ready to pray earnestly or to lend a helping hand or a sympathetic ear as each situation requires. If a colleague requests prayer about a certain matter, pray with him immediately, if possible. Caring in visible and supportive ways builds true harmony.

8. Always be tactful.

Tact is the deft handling of difficult communication. Word choice is unmistakably linked to clear communication. One man might say to his wife, "When I look into your eyes, time ceases to pass"; and another might say, "You have a face that would stop a clock." They might have the same idea in mind, but they will get different results!

Timeliness is every bit as important as tact in effective communication. When a person is tired, depressed, or troubled, it is not appropriate to offer new insights into his defects and shortcomings. Some people feel a tremendous urge to blurt out a "loving rebuke" at the moment most convenient to themselves. In reality, such people benefit themselves by "getting it off their chests" more than they benefit their unfortunate friends. Both honesty and kindness are required, and "speaking the truth in love" builds harmony on the basis of a mutual commitment to one another and to God's work.

9. Always give appropriate praise.

Praise one another both publicly and privately. Praise is the essence of motivation.

Heaviness in the heart of man maketh it stoop: but a good word maketh it glad. (Prov. 12:25)

Wise and loving Christians let others know that they are doing a good job and that their accomplishments are noticed. They are not concerned only with themselves.

10. Always make time for fellowship outside of school.

A lack of unity is a natural result of a lack of fellowship. Schools should have planned fellowship for their teachers, and teachers and administrators should spontaneously be in one another's homes and have times of fun and mutual encouragement together. This unity requires effort, but it is worth working toward. A staff should pray together and play together. These are components that hold the Christian school together.

The lofty goals of Christian education demand unity of purpose and harmony of effort. The only way to accomplish this common goal is to understand the place of each person and to practice basic principles of courtesy. When these areas are properly addressed, the school will have a unity that God can bless.

Chapter 5
The Teacher and Complaints

When a man's ways please the Lord, he maketh even his enemies to be at peace with him. (Prov. 16:7)

Let your speech be alway with grace, seasoned with salt, that ye may know how ye ought to answer every man. (Col. 4:6)

A soft answer turneth away wrath: but grievous words stir up anger. (Prov. 15:1)

That we henceforth be no more children . . . but speaking the truth in love, may grow up into him in all things, which is the head, even Christ. (Eph. 4:14-15)

Working with people means working with problems. Complaints will come; they are inevitable. Some educators find complaints debilitating. Their initial response is anger, defensiveness, or fear. These three natural responses all proceed from one source: insecurity. The security of knowing God's provision for handling complaints allows one to recognize a complaint for what it is: not a disastrous end-product but an opportunity to see the power of God in progress, perfecting His work in the lives and ministries of His saints. The effective Christian teacher will make complaints allies instead of enemies.

Attitude

Attitude is the key. Since everyone will get complaints, the Christian educator must learn to handle them in a Christ-like manner:

And the servant of the Lord must not strive; but be gentle

> *unto all men, apt to teach, patient, in meekness instructing those that oppose themselves. (II Tim. 2:24-25)*

"The servant of the Lord"

Every Christian educator is, or should be, a servant of the Lord. A servant is one who gives of himself. The world teaches lifting oneself up and winning through intimidation. Christ demonstrated stooping to serve and winning through helping others to become winners. Any Christian is a servant of the Lord if he does God's work God's way.

"Must not strive"

Strife does not build; it tears down. When a parent comes in with angry words, the teacher's angry response will build only walls, not bridges. The Christian educator's motives must be to reconcile the brother and to rectify the situation, not to prove himself right.

"But be gentle unto all men"

Gentleness requires not only a calm, even voice but also a gentle spirit. A person can have his voice under control while the red flush creeps into his face and the veins of his neck begin to stand out. True gentleness is the work of the Holy Spirit (Gal. 5:22) and is facilitated by a true servant's spirit. If the servant of God is right, he will try to help his brother see the better way. If the servant of God is wrong, he will try to correct his mistake. Either way, he is not contending for any personal pride, position, or possession. Representing the Lord, he does not feel personally threatened; therefore, he is neither fearful nor angry.

"Apt to teach"

This phrase means that the teacher must be a teacher by nature—to the very core! This person, even in the middle of a bad situation, can see an opportunity to teach the complaining party something useful for edification. Such occasions can be especially challenging when dealing with the parent who "knows it all." Nevertheless, the teacher must in all situations prove himself apt to teach.

"Patient"

A complaint usually represents a crisis, a moment of time.

However, patience reminds us that the issue or complaint is often more profound, requiring sustained effort to build and maintain bridges of cooperation. Furthermore, there are some who are inveterate complainers. No matter what the situation, they will find something to complain about. The servant of the Lord will be patient with such people, teaching and slowly winning them over. They will not change overnight, but such people can become the staunchest of allies.

"In meekness instructing"

Meekness is not weakness. A meek person is not the vacillating, self-uncertain, Caspar Milquetoast type. Moses was described as "very meek, above all men on the earth"; yet only a powerful, consistent, firm leader could have led Israel through the many oppositions she faced. Christ said, "Learn of me, for I am meek and lowly of heart"; yet He cleared the temple twice, single-handedly, and those who learned of Him looked courts and kings in the eye and stood their ground in His cause.

Meekness is power under control. The Greek word for *meek* is also used when speaking of training a horse, bringing the tremendous power of a horse under the control of his master. Perhaps some contentious, short-fused, caustic parent storms into the principal's office. The principal may have the power to expel the parent's son or daughter, demonstrating his control of the situation. Such a response would be natural—not spiritual. Better that he should demonstrate his control over himself and respond meekly by using his power to resolve the problem and restore the student, thereby glorifying God.

Parents are astonished to learn that teachers are afraid of them. Teachers are astonished to learn that *parents* are afraid of *them*. Somehow being on opposite sides of a desk has given rise to the idea of being on opposite sides of a cause. Nothing could be further from the truth. If parents and teachers in a Christian education environment do not find in each other their greatest allies in accomplishing common goals, where is such an ally to be found?

Approach

To find these allies, we must be approachable, "easy to be intreated" (James 3:17).

The first step is to *listen*—mind intent upon the person and the problem, looking the speaker in the eye, and seeking to understand not only the facts but also the motives and the causes. Listening accomplishes three important goals.

First, listening helps to defuse a tense situation. It is like letting air out of an overinflated balloon before it explodes. Listening quietly while an angry complainer hurls inaccuracies and accusations is not easy, but that is often the only way of lowering the emotional tension level to allow a reasonable exchange of information. Sometimes the complainer just "runs out of hot air" and stops. He has shot off his string of firecrackers, and he has nothing to do but to let the teacher pick up the conversation and direct it where he will.

Second, listening also tells the parent that the teacher is interested. If the parent senses that the teacher is genuinely interested in his problem, he is much more willing to work *with* the teacher rather than against him.

Finally, listening allows the educator to discern the true nature of the problem. If a parent complains, "That *teacher* gave my child too much homework. He couldn't possibly do that much homework," he is seemingly complaining about the teacher. The discerning listener will be wondering whether the problem is not the *teacher,* but the *child* and *homework.* Perhaps the child has difficulty understanding math, and the parent is frustrated because he is unable to help.

There are times and places *not* to listen to problems. The church should be a sanctuary from the pressures and problems of the day. When either the parent or the teacher brings up a problem at church, the other party may not be able to concentrate on worship. Teachers should not go to church worrying about who is going to bring up some problem. The administration should make the church off-limits to routine school business.

Classrooms, hallways, and playgrounds are not places to deal with problems. Often an impetuous parent will want to deal with some problem when he just happens to see the teacher or administrator, without regard to the privacy of the information or the concentration and time required to resolve the issue. The teacher should not say, "Not now," but should ask, "When can we make an appointment to talk about this?" Taking the initiative to set up an appointment demonstrates the teacher's concern.

After listening, the teacher should compliment. To compliment an angry parent who has just poured out a cauldron of boiling invectives is not easy. The teacher can compliment the parent for his concern for his child. He can thank him for the opportunity of working with the child and reaffirm that he does not take that responsibility lightly. He can recognize the parent's concern that the Lord's money be well spent. He can thank the parent for coming directly to him with the problem rather than spreading it around the community. With this statement and a knowing smile the teacher may have stabbed the parent because the parent *has* probably gossiped about the situation; but most people listen better with a few coals of fire heaped upon their heads.

First the teacher listens, then he compliments, and then he directs the conference toward an answer to the problem.

Answer

There are four techniques for answering complaints: question, quick answer, research and response, and correction.

Question

The Lord Jesus Christ used the question technique with the Pharisees and Sadducees. "Is it lawful to give tribute unto Caesar?" "Whose is this image and superscription?" Questioning accomplishes two goals. First, it opens the parent's understanding, perhaps to self-evident solutions or perhaps to his own lack of knowledge about what his child is doing. Second, it reveals details essential for understanding the whole problem. Always question calmly, in a nonthreatening manner. Make clear by your words, voice, face, and posture that you do not feel threatened and that your goal is only to be a help.

Quick Answer

Matters of policy require a quick answer. If a parent complains about a no-drinking policy, there is no point in asking how much the child drinks. The administrator expresses thanks that the parent has come to the right person to discuss the problem, but a right policy requires no discussion, only enforcement.

Research and Return

Sometimes the research and return technique is employed

to gain information and sometimes to gain time. When a teacher or administrator promises to research and return, he had better be sure to return! He should call back the next day, even if there is still no solution, to let the parent know that he is serious about the problem and has not forgotten about it. This technique is especially helpful when dealing with an irate parent. The additional information gained may be of help, but the value of a night's sleep and a day's perspective usually does even more good in such situations.

There are other values in simple postponement. In one case the parents believed that their child was harassed at school. He was an angel at home, but they kept hearing that he was the *other* kind of angel at school. The administrator postponed dealing with the problem and watched. One day when the boy was really tearing up the gym, his parents happened to be at the school. The administrator ran to get the parents and let them see their "angel" in action! The problem was quickly resolved. In another case, the administrator postponed the problem until the end of the school year. The parents had heard about learning disabilities, and they decided that their child had a learning disability. In reality, he was simply lazy. The administrator knew that the year before, when that child had a very strict teacher, he kept up with his work and did well. The teacher at his present grade level was not as demanding, but the teacher for the next grade was going to be another very demanding teacher. He postponed the problem, and with a change of teachers, the "learning disability" disappeared.

Correction

If the complaint is justified, the educator must admit the wrong, correct it, and make sure that it does not happen again. Pastors, teachers, and administrators are not infallible, and it is a shame if they are too proud to admit a mistake. To admit error does not detract from a person's honor; it increases it. People appreciate a leader's willingness to admit his mistakes, and they are usually eager to forgive. Teachers must be accessible. If people do not come to a teacher with problems, perhaps he is viewed as unapproachable. Such a perception will breed worse problems in time.

If the complaint is not justified, use a "soft answer," but answer honestly. "I'm sorry that problem had to come up, and

I understand how you feel about it, but I see the situation this way: therefore, this is the action I must take." The objective, kind presentation of truth is all-important because "a soft answer turneth away wrath: but grievous words stir up anger" (Prov. 15:1). The soft answer must communicate a realization of the parent's viewpoint and a compassion for his concerns, but most of all it must communicate the truth, graciously stated.

Problems are opportunities in working clothes, and complaints handled the Scriptural way can make allies instead of enemies.

Chapter 6
Teaching Strategies

Not slothful in business; fervent in spirit; serving the Lord. (Rom. 12:11)

Let all things be done decently and in order. (I Cor. 14:40)

Good teaching resulting in well-educated, Christ-like students does not "just happen." It requires planning, implementation, and evaluation of a Biblical, educationally sound strategy. Any project as vastly important as Christian education should command the best efforts of those to whom God has committed the task; there is no room for mental laziness or half-hearted engagement. The effective Christian teacher consciously develops and implements a strategy for successful teaching.

A Piece of P.I.E.

Planning

The huddle of a trained football team does not take long. The quarterback says something like "Twenty-two on blue. Break!" After a few random numbers, the ball is snapped, and the action starts. Sandlot football is not like that. The huddle lasts indefinitely. One boy says, "I'll go out for a pass," but another boy says, "Hey, you did last time. It's my turn"—and so on. When does the planning occur for the professional teams or even for trained amateurs? Planning occurs in the summer— long before the actual game. Carefully prepared game plans have been analyzed and studied. When the team hits the field, it is ready to implement those plans.

Teaching strategy is the "game plan" of the classroom, the means of accomplishing the goal. As in football, planning must begin before the teacher gets into the classroom. Admittedly, most Christian school teachers have several preparations; very few Christian schools need six sessions of the same course each day. Still, the planning *must* take place before the teacher enters the classroom. The hour is much more profitable and enjoyable for both the student and the teacher if the teacher is prepared.

Implementation

What if the quarterback is supposed to throw a fifty-yard pass, but he throws only a ten-yard toss? Or what if the lineman is supposed to push his man out of the way to create an opening, but he is tying his shoe when the ball goes into play? Advance planning is useless without effective implementation.

Some Christian school teachers are great planners, but they plan too well. They cannot effectively implement their plans in the classroom. To accomplish the desired end, they must follow their plans. "Plan your work, and work your plan," the old saying goes.

Evaluation

Do football teams evaluate? Of course! Good teams evaluate all the time—after a game, at half time, and between plays. Good players evaluate all the time. Good teachers evaluate all the time too.

Students should come with light bulbs on their heads. When a student is paying attention, a little green light should flash. When he comprehends the point the teacher is laboring to communicate, a big red light should flash. In a way, students *do* come wired with lights—their eyes. Nothing is more rewarding in teaching than seeing faces light up and heads begin to nod. Good eye contact is the primary means of in-classroom evaluation. Teachers who continually evaluate are better teachers because they are always seeking means to maintain attention and to communicate the material clearly.

The Strategy of Implementation

Effective implementation is the key to great teaching. Between the planning and the evaluation is that all-important implementation which warrants special attention.

Is a good teacher "made" or "born"? A person who is not naturally a teacher can be "made" to be a good teacher as he practices good techniques. A person who is a "born" teacher may be a good teacher by doing what comes naturally to him. However, *great* teachers are those who are both "born" teachers and "made" teachers. They are given natural gifts of the mind, spirit, and personality, and they cultivate those gifts diligently. Careful consideration and practice of good teaching strategies can help make a weak teacher become a good one and a good teacher to become a great one.

Speak with Authority

Effective teachers speak with authority. They do not "give an uncertain sound" (I Cor. 14:8). The teacher cannot be characterized by a giddy, nervous, or forced perpetual smile; he should be relaxed and natural. There are various "tricks" that a teacher can use to give an impression of speaking with authority: wearing dark, conservative clothing; varying volume, pace, and tone of voice; refusing to smile until Christmas; and the basic source of authority in teaching, knowing what he is talking about.

Most teachers in American Christian secondary schools teach subjects outside their major and minor fields of preparation, and students love to find their teachers' areas of weakness! Christian teachers should not be called upon to teach beyond their primary fields of training, but such an ideal may never be possible in many schools. However, this problem in Christian education needs correction.

There are two approaches to the problem. First, the teacher who is asked to teach a subject about which he knows nothing can graciously refuse to teach it. The following incident really happened. At a Christian school orientation, the principal asked the teachers, "Has anyone here had any German? Anybody?" His eyes scanned the group, but no hands were raised—no one dared scratch his nose! "Mr. Smith! Didn't you take German in high school? Didn't I see that on your records? Good, then you can teach German in the high school for us." Mr. Smith, who had had one year of high school German, should have graciously refused on the basis that he was unqualified to teach German. Administrators are human, too, and some will take the path of least resistance. Too often they cease praying and seeking alternatives. As a result, the school misses the blessing that the Lord wanted to send.

The teacher pushed beyond the area of his expertise has a second option: he can *become* an authority. Anyone who has been through four years of college should have the intellectual skills to approach an unfamiliar topic, discern the principles, and master the details; but it takes time and planning *in advance.* The teacher who is always preparing the night before is in trouble if something unexpected comes up. It takes only one instance of fumbling uncertainty for the teacher's authority in that field to be weakened for the rest of the year.

Teaching with Enthusiasm

How do students become excited about history, English, or math? They become excited by having teachers who are excited about their subject matter. If the teacher is not excited about the subject, the students most certainly will not be. Excitement is contagious, and it is based more on the attitude of the teacher than on the subject matter. There are no uninteresting subjects, only uninterested people.

The same is true of getting students excited about serving the Lord in full-time Christian service. Students become excited about becoming pastors, missionaries, or Christian school teachers when they see examples in teachers, pastors, and missionaries who are joyfully serving the Lord and who are excited about what they are doing. The Christian school teacher has a part in shaping the minds of the next generation, those that will take up the torch of the gospel. He should thank the Lord for that! The Christian school teacher should be excited about his subject matter and his profession.

Just before a big game, the coach goes into the locker room with energy and enthusiasm and says, "Come on, guys, let's go! This is the big game. Give it your all!" The coach is all fired up, and the team gets all fired up. Principals need to be like coaches. They need to get their teachers fired up about their mission, and teachers need to pass the vision on to their students.

A teacher should be tired at the end of a day of teaching. A large expenditure of emotional energy should be noticeable. Enthusiastic teaching is draining physically and emotionally but is worthwhile. The Biblical principle of sowing and reaping contains a promise:

He which soweth sparingly shall reap also sparingly; and he which soweth bountifully shall reap also bountifully. (II Cor. 9:6)

If we are called to invest our lives in teaching, we should invest at a high rate of "interest"; that is, we should be interested in our teaching and gain the maximum return on our investment. The dividends of enthusiastic teaching are issued both here and hereafter; these are the real "paychecks" of Christian teaching.

Reinforce Student Behavior

Praise is the best reinforcement of all. A little bit of praise from the teacher goes a long way to encourage the positive and to erode the negative behaviors in students.

Both positive and negative reinforcements (rewards and punishments) are needed. Christian schools, however, place too much emphasis on the negative and neglect the positive. What do students assume when "Johnny" is called to the office? Is something disastrous about to happen to Johnny there? Sometimes students should be sent to the office or kept after class for *praise*. Keep them guessing! Use both positive and negative reinforcement.

Appeal to Students' Interests and Abilities

The teacher needs to find out what students are interested in and take part in their interests. He should go to their recitals, ball games, and concerts. He should show an interest in student activities and talk with the students about what they like to talk about: cars, sports, boys, girls, etc. How can the teacher use classroom illustrations that appeal to student interests if he never spends time talking to students, finding out what their interests are?

A businessman trying to gain a new account will find out what his potential client is interested in, read about it, and look for an opportunity to converse on that topic. He acts with the ulterior motive of fostering a new account, and there is nothing wrong with the tactic. Should not the Christian teacher, attempting to influence lives permanently, be every bit as subtle and wise as the businessman attempting to make money?

If there is a secret to working with young people, it is this: care. Simple and genuine care is the magic formula for success with children and teens. They know if the teacher loves them. Students at any age level can detect when the teacher cares, and they will respond.

Teachers must also tailor the lesson to suit the students' ability levels. Every classroom has students achieving on a number of levels, with the majority at medium level. The teacher appeals primarily to the average achievers, but he should provide some extra challenges for the sharp ones and some extra practice exercises for the slow ones. Such variety helps the slow ones catch up and keeps the sharp ones from getting bored.

Sadly, the tendency is to neglect advanced students. Teachers overwhelmed with the task of keeping the majority working while tending to the needs of the stragglers forget about the smart ones. Teachers contend that the above-average students will get the basic material by themselves. Meanwhile, these brighter students become bored, sour, and rebellious. If the teacher does not keep them challenged, they will find something on their own to meet their interests and abilities, and what they find will probably *not* be what the teacher would have chosen. If the teacher does not have a plan, the students will! Rarely can all levels of the same material be taught, but there must be some extra or alternative books, reports, projects— something designed just for the gifted and talented students.

Treat Big Ideas Simply

Teachers make big ideas simple by reducing them to their component elements. A thick, sumptuous steak is not swallowed whole, but it is reduced to bite-sized pieces which can be eaten individually. Just to say "Write a research paper" is not sufficient. Students can choke on such an assignment. Assignments need to be broken down into the component parts, such as choosing a topic, limiting the topic, checking the library for available materials, note taking, etc.

Teachers also make big ideas simple by using verbal illustrations. The goal is to take students from the familiar to the unfamiliar, from what they understand to what is new to them, precept by precept. A teacher should provide many examples, illustrations, and explanations arranged in an orderly sequence as he makes big ideas simple.

Exercise Control over the Learning Situation

Control is far more important than discipline, although discipline is very important. Students will not learn if they are running around the room. One of the best means of classroom control is the control of the *rate of learning*. The teacher should keep the class moving. He should know where he is going (careful planning), and he should be ready to move on to new material when the students have grasped the lesson already presented (continuous evaluation). This control requires overpreparation. The teacher who is barely prepared to make it through the class time is in trouble when he ends up with fifteen minutes of dead time. Remember, if the teacher does not have a plan, the students will! When the students are challenged with interesting, appropriate material, they will be less likely to get into mischief.

The teacher, not the curriculum nor the lowest ability level of the students, sets the pace in the classroom. A curriculum is a valuable tool, but it is not Holy Writ. A good teacher will know where he is headed, will keep the class moving, and will always have something more for them.

Go to Parents and Students

Who is ultimately responsible for the education of young people? Parents, when kept well-informed, are one of the greatest assets a Christian school can have. They care; they love their children, and they pay tuition to get them the best Christian education possible. Parents usually want to work with the school to resolve problems, whether spiritual, academic, or social. However, if most of the students are lost young people with unsaved parents, they will be unable to comprehend the goals of the school, and they will be understandably unwilling to cooperate.

Teachers often fear going to parents because of some actual or imagined bad experience. Parents are surprised to hear of this reluctance because *they* are afraid of the teachers because of all their education. However, teachers who have learned to go to parents early find that those parents are their best earthly asset in ministering to the students.

The teacher should be going to students too. In addition to showing interest in what they are interested in, the teacher and administrator should put "spiritual pressure" on students.

The teacher might approach a student like this: "Phil, you're a leader. You really have potential to go places. The only question is whether you are going to use it for the Lord or for the world. I'm going to be tough on you. I'm going to teach you to channel that ability because you can be a real champion for the Lord Jesus Christ, and I want you to serve the Lord, not the world. I want you to know that I am praying for you. If there is any way I can help you, just let me know." He would then confront that student each time he expresses a bad attitude or behaves improperly. After a little while, one of two things will happen: the student will either get right or get out. It is discouraging when students respond negatively to spiritual pressure, but such pressure is necessary in showing them that there really are spiritual absolutes.

Y Use Audiovisuals

If it *must* fit the acrostic, this section might be titled "You Use Audiovisuals"; but whatever the title, the effective teacher will use audiovisuals. Audio-visual resources include overhead projectors, films, records, handouts, and wall charts. Some teachers complain about the lack of funds for these aids. However, we should not neglect the audio-visual tools with which all teachers come equipped: hands, voice, face, gestures, and so on. Too many teachers are tied to their podiums and drone on in a sedative monotone, lulling their students into the sleepy land of nonthought.

Too often, expensive audio-visual equipment lies unused or is used in the most meager, unimaginative ways because teachers do not take the preparation time that these tools require. Before complaining about a lack of materials, the teacher should first see that he is using well the audiovisuals that God has given him; then he is in a position to pray for more.

The Evaluation That Counts

The effective Christian teacher is continually going through the cycle of planning, implementation, and evaluation. It is not a monotonous circle, but an ever-ascending spiral as the teacher rises to new heights of ability and success. One day, when the final evaluation is done, that teacher will hear the Lord say, "Well done, thou good and faithful servant: thou hast been faithful over a few things, I will make thee ruler over many things: enter thou into the joy of thy lord." (Matt. 25:21)

Chapter 7
Teaching by Principle

A scorner seeketh wisdom, and findeth it not: but knowledge is easy unto him that understandeth. (Prov. 14:6)

For precept must be upon precept, precept upon precept; line upon line, line upon line; here a little and there a little. (Isa. 28:10)

If there were a way to make learning easier and permanent, perhaps we would all be millionaires. Actually, there is a way to make learning easier and more permanent, but it is often neglected: teaching by principle. Individual facts are important, but a student will never understand the subject completely nor be able to apply what he has learned until he understands the principles underlying the facts. The teacher who imparts this kind of understanding makes his students succeed in courses they never could master before. It is that kind of teacher who restores a student's confidence and builds his self-esteem and whom students fondly recall throughout their lives. The effective Christian teacher teaches by principle.

Definition

A *principle* is a general truth from which specific applications can be made. Teaching by principle stands in contrast to teaching facts only; it requires teaching general truths in addition to teaching specific facts. These general truths are not an additional unit nor even additional lines of lecture notes. Rather, they are the focal point of *explanation* to which all teaching refers. The teacher first organizes his lessons around these principles; then he clearly states *how* points are related to each other.

He shows cause-and-effect relationships. For example, under-lying the dates of the Civil War is a set of facts about sectionalism, slavery, and economics that focused all the pressures that caused the war and dictated its direction and duration. Another set of truths about greed, power, and pride lies deeper and explains the sectionalism, slavery, and some of the darker features of the economics. This level of explanation traces the causes all the way to James 4:1, "From whence come wars and fightings among you? Come they not hence, even of your lusts that war in your members?"

Teaching by principle provides the tools for *applying the knowledge* in new situations. The student who understands the causes of the Civil War all the way down to the James 4:1 level can see those same forces at work in other wars and in his own interpersonal relations; he can apply the principle to history and daily living.

Biblical Basis

No teaching method is valid or ultimately productive unless it conforms to Biblical principles and practice. Certainly nothing could be more Biblical than the method of teaching by principle.

Christ taught by principle through parables. When accused of associating with sinners, Christ told three stories in Luke 15 about lost things—the lost sheep, the lost coin, and the lost son. All three parables had one basic point: we must be about the business of seeking the lost. In Matthew 6 the Lord spoke of the Father's care of the lilies of the field and the fowls of the air with this intent: God will take care of His own as they order their priorities in His plan. He could not have listed every possible need, but the references to stature, raiment, and food are basic and include every conceivable need in every period of history. The Father watches and cares.

The Bible is a book of principles. A mere rule book would become outdated with each new technology or fad. God did not list every modern substance, or those yet future, with which people defile their minds and bodies; but He dealt specifically with wine and established the principle that we are not to be brought under the power of any substance.

Levels of Learning

One basic sequence is characteristic of learning. The steps

sometimes occur simultaneously and sometimes very slowly, depending upon the background of the learner and the nature of the material, but each step is essential. The problem encountered in classroom education is usually not the attempt to skip levels, but a complacency with low-level learning.

Exposure

The most basic task, of course, is to present the material to the student in a logical sequence on a level that he can comprehend.

Activation

Too often the teacher stops with mere exposure. "The good students will get it; let the lazy ones flunk!" This attitude does not demonstrate the heart of a true teacher. The true teacher consciously works to activate the students' mental engagement with the material. Often the activation stage is initiated in the form of motivation or interest arousal before the exposure to the facts begins. The effective teacher encourages thinking by skillful use of questions, discussion, and thought-provoking illustrations. He may even play the devil's advocate, proposing the opposite of what he is trying to teach in order to engage the learners in explaining, proving, or defending the correct position. The teacher who uses this method must be sure that he clarifies the correct position at the end. Because students' attention comes and goes, he is in danger of being severely misunderstood if a student tunes in only for the devil's advocate part.

Comprehension

Comprehension is seeing all the facts fit together into a larger whole. The student sees that all the little parts of the picture are important.

Most Christian elementary school students excel in math facts. Nationally, Christian schools do well in the computation skills, but there is a dramatic drop in the achievement scores for the upper levels of math. The reason is that students memorize facts, but they do not understand the principles. Students can memorize that $3 \times 3 = 9$ without knowing *why* it equals 9. Elementary teachers need to use those basic illustrations of multiplication such as three cookies with three chocolate chips each, totaling nine chocolate chips. Such understanding is foundational. Students need to see that multiplication is a faster means of adding and that addition is an abbreviation of counting. They need to understand the commutative property, identity elements, and other concepts of numbers, or they are set back several stages in the process of learning in upper-level math courses where memorization is not enough. In every area of human endeavor there comes a point where memorization of facts is not enough, where understanding and application are necessary for advancement.

Conviction

Conviction is the level of belief. The goal is application of the learned material; but before the students can apply the material beyond the classroom, they must comprehend the necessary elements, and they must believe that what they have learned will work. Developing topic sentences into paragraphs, reading for edification, or meditating upon Scripture are examples of applying learned materials.

Application

Students will apply principles that they understand, but they may not always see how a principle applies. The teacher should illustrate applications in his teaching and, as much as possible, provide for application in classroom practice and testing.

The Christian educator should never avoid the lower levels of learning and pass directly to comprehension, conviction, and application. Students cannot comprehend a principle unless they have been exposed to the facts and have actively considered them. First the student is exposed to the material. Then he begins thinking about it, understanding it, believing it, and finally, utilizing it. Factual memorization and drill alone are not adequate education, but they *are* essential steps toward the application of principles.

The teacher's goal is to train students to become thinkers. America as a whole, as well as much of the Christian community, is characterized by a passive, puppet-minded, television-trained mentality. For this reason many Christians are unable to analyze and apply Scripture practically. If young people are not learning to think at school, they should not be expected to develop skills of analysis and discernment suddenly when confronted with spiritual decisions.

Every student should be required to pass algebra because of the high level of thinking it requires. Literature courses are also ideal training ground for critical thinking. Students must learn to read with discernment. It is not enough to read only works by Bible-believing authors. No matter who the author is, students must learn to read with discernment, seeing each subject from God's perspective. Christians are to be followers of God, not of any man, no matter how great a Christian he may be. Students must learn to discern truth from error for themselves, and the skills learned in the classroom can sharpen that ability.

Wisdom

The implications for the Christian are clear and compelling: he must apply the principles of what has been learned. The Christian life is not a narrow segment of the Christian's day; it is his whole life. "For the Christian there is no difference between the secular and the sacred," said Dr. Bob Jones, Sr. "For the Christian all things are sacred. All ground is holy ground, and every bush a burning bush." Just as some secular educators define education as the acquisition of *useful* knowledge, the Christian should likewise concentrate on learning to prepare better to serve and worship the Lord.

Wisdom, as every junior-aged Sunday school child knows, is knowing how to use knowledge; it is the *application* level of learning.

The book of Proverbs continually exhorts the Christian to reach that level of attainment:

The proverbs of Solomon the son of David, king of Israel; To know wisdom and instruction; to perceive the words of understanding; To receive the instruction of wisdom, justice, and judgment, and equity; To give subtilty to the simple, to the young man knowledge and discretion. A wise man will hear, and will increase learning; and a man of understanding shall attain unto wise counsels. (1:1-5)

Happy is the man that findeth wisdom, and the man that getteth understanding. (3:13)

Over one hundred other references to wisdom and understanding are found in Proverbs. God stresses that "wisdom is the principal thing; therefore get wisdom: and with all thy getting get understanding" (Prov. 4:7).

Wisdom is the academic goal of Christian education. The overall goal is that the student become Christ-like, and the academic corollary of that is wisdom. This goal is not greatly different from the secular educators' goal of "useful knowledge" except that the term *wisdom* implies to the Christian that the principles involved are Biblically sound.

"Why's" of Learning

Does everyone want a classroom full of Sweet Susies? Sweet Susie always says, "Yes, sir. Anything you say, sir." Never a question. Never a problem. But then there is Terrible Tim. For every rule he has to have an explanation. He always has a question, and he wants to know the "why" for everything. "Because I said so" is not enough for him.

Granted, the fact that an authority has spoken is sufficient to command instant obedience; and, granted, a first-grader does not have to understand why broccoli is good for him before he eats it, but we should welcome the Terrible Tims, and we should satisfy the inquiring minds. These are the leaders of tomorrow. These are the ones who will recognize, examine, and refute the encroachments of error and defend—with understanding—the right.

As children grow, they should be given, as much as they are able to comprehend, the principles behind the facts of nature and the *why's* behind the rules of successful Christian living. A student who never understands never assimilates. Although he may conform to the outward expectations of faith and practice, they are never his own, and he immediately forsakes them upon leaving the environment where they are required.

Whether teaching phonics, physics, or the dynamics of faith, the key is in the application. Therefore, Christian teachers must teach by principle.

Chapter 8
Teaching Through Testing

Give therefore thy servant an understanding heart to judge thy people, that I may discern between good and bad: for who is able to judge this thy so great a people? And the speech pleased the Lord, that Solomon had asked this thing. (I Kings 3:9-10)

But strong meat belongeth to them that are of full age, even those who by reason of use have their senses exercised to discern both good and evil. (Heb 5:14)

'Twas the day before testing, and all through the school
Not a student was stirring; they kept every rule.

Students can be amazingly attentive and cooperative the day before testing. After study sheets have been given out, students hustle to get every little bit of information that the teacher will share before the test. Sometimes the teacher not only reviews for the test but also actually gives the page number and paragraph from which each test question will come. Too many teachers rely on study sheets, allowing students to memorize the factual information the day before the test. The progression runs similar to this:

1. Poor students rarely listen in class or take notes.
2. The class is given study sheets before the test.
3. Students listen very attentively to get all the facts on the study sheet.
4. Students memorize all the facts on the study sheet.
5. Poor students write on the test sheet the facts that they memorized the night before.
6. Some students then forget the facts that they memorized.

7. Some students become disobedient, disrespectful, and uninterested, and some do not listen or take notes until the next study sheet is given out.

Regrettably, this procedure is practiced in many Christian schools. Students are not challenged to think, analyze, or evaluate. They are forced only to drill, memorize, and regurgitate. Teaching and testing that focus only on the facts are not training the students properly. Higher levels of intellectual skill can be taught through testing.

Purpose of Each Question Type

Throughout the American Christian school movement a common weakness exists in teacher-made tests. Most tests are designed to measure only the memorizing ability of students, not the discerning ability. Many students in our Christian schools study only to take tests. However, Christian schools should be preparing students for life through the tests that they take. Students will not automatically strive for understanding and application without an emphasis on those higher mental skills. It is important that teachers use a variety of questions in their testing program because each type of question has a different purpose.

1. Fill-in-the-blank

Fill-in-the-blank questions are designed to see how well students can memorize and recall very important factual information; students must have total recall to answer this type of question. The material that students should recall in later school days or for years ahead should be memorized and tested. Names of places, dates, and other such factual material are the kinds of information that teachers desire the students to recall.

2. Matching

In matching questions, a list of information is on one side of the page with a list of possible answers on the other side. Normally, there are more possible answers than there are questions to be matched. A student cannot therefore choose an answer simply by the elimination process. This type of question causes a student to recall material by recognizing facts and matching them with other key facts or thoughts. Since some thinking and discerning skills are necessary, information which a teacher desires students to know from observation should be tested in this manner. Thus, the student is not forced to have the material memorized as with the fill-in-the-blank question.

3. Multiple Choice

With multiple choice questions, an incomplete statement or a question may be answered by one or more of several possible choices. The students must evaluate each possible choice and determine which choice best completes the thought or answers the question. Sometimes one of the choices will be "all of the above" or any combination of the four choices (both A and B, both A and C, etc.). These questions force students to higher thought processes than do the fill-in-the-blank or matching ones.

4. True/False

True/false statements require the students to determine whether a statement is completely true or at least partially false. The student must evaluate every part of the statement to make certain that not even one word causes the entire statement to be false. Sometimes students are required not only to answer true or false but also to correct the false portion of the statement to make it true. Some teachers have even developed the multiple true/false question which divides the statement into part A and part B. The students are then required to determine whether (1) parts A and B are both true, (2) parts A and B are both false, (3) part A is true, but part B is false, or (4) part A is false, but part B is true.

True/false statements are many times considered to be "tricky." To make the correct choice, students must have a thorough understanding of the material and *must analyze each point* of the statement to verify that it is true. Of course, it is possible in a simple true/false section for students to guess and answer some questions correctly. However, the corrected true/false question and the multiple true/false question help to limit this possibility.

5. The Short-Answer Question

Short-answer questions require a student to *express himself* in a sentence or two when answering a question. It is impossible for a student to answer short-answer questions properly without having a thorough understanding of the material requested. A short-answer question should be used when a teacher desires to make sure that students understand the material and have not merely memorized it.

6. *Essay Questions*

Essay questions are the fear of students and teachers alike because they require *analytical and organized thinking.* Teachers do not like essay questions because they require thought in constructing and grading; yet they should be given regularly. It is extremely important that students learn to express themselves logically and properly. Verbal communication skills are very important, and teachers should design essay questions so that students can state what they have learned. Such questions not only will help teachers to be objective in their grading but also will cause students to be specific in their answers rather than vague and rambling.

Good tests are made by using a variety of these test questions. Every teacher should evaluate his goals in giving the test and then write questions that will accomplish these goals. If the teacher desires to see whether the students have learned certain factual material, he should use all fill-in-the-blank and matching questions. However, if a teacher desires the students to think and analyze, then a mixture of multiple choice, true/false, short-answer, and essay questions should be used. Not every test should be the same. Every test should be designed to develop and examine the exact skills the teacher has purposed to teach.

One of the major testing problems in Christian schools is the use of "prepackaged" tests from textbook publishers. Even though these tests help eliminate work for the teacher and make grading easy, they are not good for the students. A teacher never teaches the material exactly the way the textbook presents it. Tests should be designed to evaluate the material the teacher has emphasized. A teacher who uses prepackaged tests will have a tendency to "teach the test" rather than to teach the subject. Most prepackaged tests are very fact-oriented rather than understanding-oriented. Using them will cause us to develop students who memorize and then forget, rather than students who understand and subsequently apply.

Standardized Achievement Tests

Achievement testing needs to be a part of every Christian school's testing program. Achievement tests should be given at the same time each year to help evaluate student progress from year to year. Test results for an individual student and for classes should be plotted through the years. Evaluations are necessary to ascertain that students are receiving a year's instruction in each calendar year. Their progress can be evaluated by plotting percentile scores as shown in Figure 1. A student or class whose percentile score goes up each year is making more than a year's progress in each calendar year. However, if the chart shows that a student or class's percentile score is going down each year, they are not obtaining the desired year's instruction within a given school year. If a school is not testing student achievement annually, these types of evaluations cannot be made.

Figure 8.1

Grade-equivalent scores can show whether a student is above or below average but *should not* be used to report achievement test results. They can be easily misunderstood. Some parents may believe that their child is doing fifth-grade work when he is in the third grade because of a grade-equivalent score. It is foolish to have parents believe that a student in the third grade is really doing fifth-grade work.

Percentile scores are more meaningful to report. These scores show how a student ranks within the population of all students taking the achievement test. A percentile score of 70 shows that a student is doing better than 70% of the population that took the test. A percentile score of 50 shows that a student is doing better than 50% of the population. If a similar population of students takes the achievement test at each level, a student who is progressing normally should never decrease in percentile score but should always maintain or improve his percentile score. The percentile score has some true meaning which can be expressed; the grade-equivalent score can be misunderstood or even damaging.

The achievement test can also show weaknesses in curriculum and in teachers. If the administrator notices that achievement test scores for a particular grade level consistently drop (See Figure 2.), he can assume that there is a problem with learning in that classroom. This problem could be due to a curriculum which fails to cover adequately the necessary material or to a teacher who fails to teach it adequately. In either case, a thorough evaluation should be conducted to determine the problem. The analysis should be based on class averages, not on individual scores, because individual scores commonly fluctuate ten to twenty percentile points because of illness, emotional upset, or other factors not related to real learning.

Figure 8.2

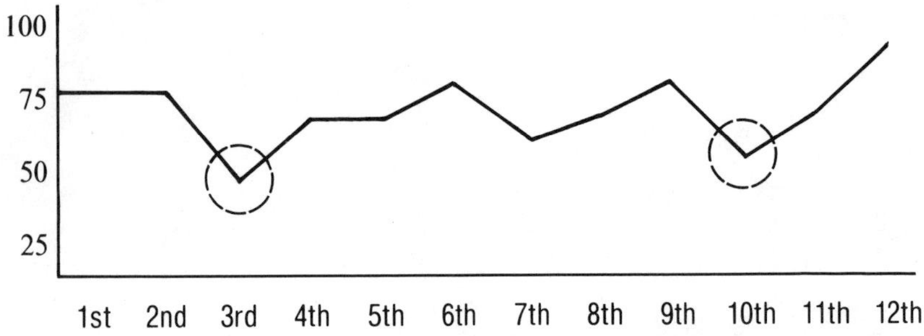

Every school needs to have a testing plan and procedure and an established standardized testing program. Teachers should be required to develop their own tests that will be effective in training the students in the higher intellectual skills. Administrators can work with the teachers to help them develop this type of test.

Testing should reflect the goals of teaching as it measures the accomplishment of those goals. If the Christian school's goal is to develop young people who can analyze, reason, and relate, then the testing program should reflect that goal. Although they require both time and effort, such teaching and testing will enrich and strengthen students for a lifetime.

Chapter 9
Teaching by Motivation

And let us consider one another to provoke unto love and to good works. (Heb. 10:24)

Whether therefore ye eat, or drink, or whatsoever ye do, do all to the glory of God. (I Cor. 10:31)

The need to motivate students comes second only to the need for classroom discipline. Long after the battle for classroom control ceases, the quest for effective means of motivation typically persists. The best teacher shows the depth and persistence of concern that form the foundation of good motivation.

Motivation simply combines the forces that make people choose, continue in, and complete any task. Motivation touches the spirit and the soul of man. God commands Christians to provoke (motivate) one another to right attitudes (love) and right actions (good works) in the context of Christian fellowship: "Not forsaking the assembling of ourselves together . . . but exhorting [a form of motivation] one another" (Heb. 10:25). Not only academic success but also spiritual growth depend on proper motivation. Teachers must, therefore, motivate their students to achieve the goal of Christian education: Christ-likeness.

Ultimately, the desire to glorify God should motivate Christians. The Bible admonishes, "Whether therefore ye eat, or drink, or whatsoever ye do, do all to the glory of God" (I Cor. 10:31). However, most of the motivation that takes place in the classroom begins externally with the teacher rather than internally with the student. Therefore, the teacher must continually use external means of motivation to encourage student achievement, and he must pray that the Holy Spirit will internally motivate the student to want to please God. This internal motivation to please God will keep young people doing right and maturing many years after they leave the Christian school.

Needs That Motivate

A. H. Maslow, an authority on educational motivation, presented the following hierarchy of needs basic to motivation:

Figure 9.1

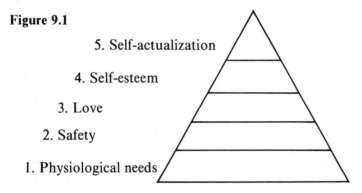

5. Self-actualization

4. Self-esteem

3. Love

2. Safety

1. Physiological needs

The most basic needs are *physiological*, that is, the needs for food and shelter. Few students in our Christian schools lack these basic needs; nevertheless, students will not respond unless their physiological needs are met first.

Safety is the second basic need. We need to provide a safe, nonthreatening environment, free not only from physical danger but also from social embarrassment. No student will achieve properly if he fears physical or mental danger. The classroom and the teacher alike must communicate safety in order to motivate the student to learn.

Love involves both acceptance and concern. The caring teacher's power to change lives is proverbial in American education. Most of us can recall a warm, personal, caring teacher who influenced our lives and who represents our idea of what a good teacher ought to be. Students who realize that the teacher cares will much more likely follow that teacher's lead into the unknown ("hard") and the unfamiliar ("boring"). The Lord Jesus

Christ said to His disciples, "If ye love me, keep my commandments" (John 14:15), but that was said only after the analysis of His love for them: "having loved his own which were in the world, he loved them unto the end" (13:1).

Self-esteem comes from recognizing God's purpose in creating us and then resting contentedly in Him. We preserve and enhance self-esteem by avoiding disaster and achieving success: the daily challenges of the classroom. Proper self-esteem does not produce arrogant pride but rather a confidence that "I am fearfully and wonderfully made" (Ps. 139:14). Essential for service, self-esteem produces the confidence that God is working in our lives, and it emboldens us to say, "Here am I, send me."

As self-esteem must rest on the Scriptural foundation of the value of the individual, so must *self-actualization* rest on an adequate picture of what God wants each person to be and to become. That picture has two main divisions: the universal and the specific. Some Scriptural goals apply to all Christians, such as "Be ye holy; for I am holy" (I Pet. 1:16). Other important features of God's plan specify developing the unique gifts and talents that He has invested in each of His children. First Peter 4:11 tells us to develop our gifts "as of the ability which God giveth." As Dr. Bob Jones, Sr., said, "It is a sin to do less than your best." Some of the teacher's more exciting experiences come as he leads students into recognizing and developing their God-given talents.

Maslow's hierarchy of needs stresses that one level of need must be satisfied to some degree before a person can attain to the next level of need. In reality, man is not guided simply by his basic needs. Yet, under most circumstances, the hierarchy holds true. For instance, sleep, a physiological need, can interfere with loftier goals, such as protecting self-esteem by staying awake in class. Although any situation can and does occur in our classrooms, most of our daily work does not concern the extreme of meeting physiological and safety needs. The needs of love, self-esteem, and self-actualization, however, must figure into the teacher's daily strategy for motivation.

Internal and External Motivation

Internal motivation comes from within the individual rather than from outside. For example, the desire to complete a book to see what happens rather than to make a good grade on a book report comes from internal motivation. Internal motivation excels external motivation because it does not depend upon the teacher. Whereas one teacher may excel in providing motivation, another may not. If learning is to continue as a lifetime process, it must have a seat of motivation within the learner.

But *external motivation* is an absolute essential. The teacher cannot reach the student's internal drives but can work through external methods to produce an internal result. A child is naturally curious, but usually that curiosity has been stifled to some degree by the time the student reaches school. By the time he enters high school, he may have had so many negative experiences that he has an aversion for, rather than an attraction to, the unknown. The teacher must find ways to stimulate that natural curiosity. A child has natural desires to be and to become—the desires for self-esteem and self-actualization—but he is also naturally lazy. The teacher must direct the student into learning experiences with sufficient pleasure and fulfillment to carry the student past his natural laziness when he moves out of the teacher's sphere of influence.

The Christian teacher understands that the Holy Spirit can touch the spirit and the soul of man; only He can directly influence the seat of internal motivation. The teacher must work on the outside and must pray that God would work on the inside, "for we are labourers together with God" (I Cor. 3:9).

Positive and Negative Motivation

Are both rewards and punishments good and necessary? Without a doubt! Those who look down on negative motivation ignore the fact that foolishness is "bound in the heart of a child"; in other words, it is tightly bound by natural depravity. To drive this foolishness from man, God Himself uses positive and negative motivators. He gives blessings, crowns, and rewards to the faithful Christian and conviction and chastisement to the unfaithful. The greatest positive motivation in the universe is heaven, and the greatest negative motivation is hell.

One danger in motivation comes from an overemphasis on the negative. Positive motivators require more work and imagination, but they offer more lasting results. They more readily meet the needs of love, self-esteem, and self-actualization.

Negatives are necessary, but they should not exist to the exclusion of positives. Furthermore, every negative should have a corresponding positive. If the teacher uses demerits, he should also recognize those with few or no demerits. If he uses punishment for incomplete homework, he should also reward those who consistently complete it. Positive teachers get the best results.

Fear motivates. Fear of demerits, of spankings, of expulsion—these external motivators can make students conform to the rules until they graduate. But if students do not possess the internal motivation to bring glory to God, the motivation will flag and the young person will fail. The Christian school teacher must keep his eyes on the ultimate goal: developing students with an inward desire to glorify God.

Techniques of Motivation

Every teacher can have the power to motivate. Not a mysterious gift bestowed upon a random few, motivation is both an art and a science. It is a science in that certain basic principles are always true. It is an art in that skill in applying those principles grows with practice.

As the teacher yields himself to be what God wants him to be and diligently seeks to do what God wants him to do, he will find that he grows in the ability to motivate his students. "It is God which worketh in you both to will and to do of his good pleasure" (Phil. 2:13). Anything God calls us to do, He enables us to do; Christians "can do all things through Christ," who strengthens them (Phil. 4:13).

A wise teacher does everything within his power to make his classroom a place for learning. Although he cannot directly produce a desire for learning, he can provide an environment conducive to learning just as a grower of rare and fragile plants provides a greenhouse environment to promote those plants' natural growth in the midst of a hostile climate.

Love, warmth, and *support*—these terms describe the teacher's relationship to his students. Because love is such a deep need, students will respond readily to a teacher who loves them. The teacher must first receive this love for his students as a gift from God, and he must subsequently demonstrate it. Whether he teaches kindergarten or senior high, a teacher expresses love in very much the same way. Looking a student in the eyes and using his first name communicates a warm, personal relationship. Talking to students about their interests and praying with them about their needs creates a powerful bond of mutual affection.

Students should also learn to support one another. The teacher should never allow students to laugh at others' mistakes. A student, especially as he gets older, needs real courage to raise his hand and answer a question in class. He lays his ego on the line and risks that dreaded titter of laughter that crushes the spirit. The teacher should strive, as much as possible, to make every answer a right answer. He can pick up on a part of the answer that was right and build upon that; or, at the very least, he can say, "Hmm, that shows some thought." Alertness to emotional needs allows the teacher to build a warm, safe atmosphere for learning.

Control is an essential complement to love. Just as the father who loves his son chastens him early, so does the teacher who loves his students. Students want consistent, purposeful boundaries. Effective classroom control frees students from much of the harassment of others and helps them to suppress their own natural inclination to drift away from the work at hand. Consistent control allows a student to develop habits of work and attentiveness that become part of his self-image.

Freedom does not contradict but rather complements the requirement of control. As a student grows, he should be allowed to make more of his own decisions—within clearly defined boundaries. In the primary grades, the teacher might prescribe exactly what science project each student should do. In the upper elementary grades, the teacher might give a list of five projects to choose from. The junior high student might be allowed to select any project of his own devising, subject to the teacher's prior approval; and the senior high student would have the same allowance, but with a broader range of approval.

Freedom of choice, however, includes the freedom to suffer because of wrong choices. The senior high student who chooses to build a low-power laser may find that he has to invest long hours and a certain amount of money to complete his project. The teacher must see that students do not make mistakes having long-range consequences; on the other hand, he must also remember that the little mistakes of life are sometimes the best teachers.

Respect grows upon the foundation of love, promotes self-esteem, and encourages students to go onward to new levels of accomplishment. Even a kindergarten student recognizes ridicule, sarcasm, and avoidance. Respect is a two-way street, and the teacher who gives respect will more likely receive it from his students. The student who believes that his teacher respects his worth as part of God's plan will more likely apply himself to his work.

Anybody thrills to a *challenge*, but it must be a challenge within his reach. Some students dread any challenge because they have had so many defeats in the past. Challenge needs to come with encouragement. Most Christian schools have high academic standards, but few schools know how to transfer excellent academics from the teacher to the student. Wise teachers will, therefore, challenge their students with the subject matter. The teacher must then be ready to help as the students need help. Students can become excited about meeting a challenge when that challenge comes with encouragement and appropriate amounts of help.

Nothing succeeds like *success.* This statement is true whether the success comes by ordinary means or with help from the teacher. Nobody enjoys coming to help classes, but those classes are the "intensive care unit" for injured confidence. The sooner the student attains success in a given problem area, the easier the teacher's job of motivation will be in every area. Therefore, all learning should follow logically arranged steps, and the teacher should constantly look for the point at which he has lost the class or an individual. He should not let his students flounder but should go to their rescue as soon as possible.

The teacher can often ensure success, particularly when students do individual projects. The teacher should consider those students who have trouble in a given area and direct their choices accordingly. A student who is not especially strong in his research and writing skills should be directed toward a topic in which he will have access to an abundance of easily understood material. For example, a high school senior should be directed away from a report on the psycho-linguistic roots of the imagery of William Butler Yeats and toward a report on the major themes of Yeats's poetry.

Variety is an important motivator because anything grows stale after a long enough period of repetition. Added to the basic recipe of good order and comfortable routine, a dash of variety, surprise, and adventure solidifies abstract learning experiences. A film, a field trip, or a discussion can break the routine. The younger the student, the shorter the period of time that he can concentrate on one task. The teacher should move from one topic to another and punctuate his presentations with a variety of methods. An elementary history lesson of twenty minutes can easily incorporate five techniques: writing notes on the chalkboard, reading aloud from the book, discussing photographs in the book, asking review questions, and asking thought questions.

Finally, *enthusiasm* helps to create an environment conducive to learning. When the teacher enjoys his material and believes that it is important, the student will likely share that excitement. Teachers convey enthusiasm by the voice— variations of pace, volume, and emphasis—by facial expression, and by bodily movement. The teacher should let his face react and his hands move naturally. If the teacher can find some features of the material that excite him, the students are much more likely to be motivated also.

Pressure for Learning

Providing a place for learning is largely a matter of being sure that existing motivations are allowed to develop naturally. *Pressures,* both positive and negative, change natural tendencies. Some pressures, like punishments, inhibit natural bad tendencies, such as lying or dishonesty. Other pressures, like rewards, stimulate the good, such as the desire to accomplish a worthwhile goal. The ultimate goal of any pressure is to stimulate internal motivation.

Punishments are powerful motivators. An effective punishment can motivate a student to move away from one action and toward another. The student must see the punishment as linked to his own wrong choice, not to the teacher's mood or whim. Students must, therefore, clearly understand the conditions that produce punishment. They must also understand that punishment will be consistent, for students despise inconsistency in authorities.

Any consideration of punishment must also include *rewards*. The existence of 101 New Testament references to rewards should convince us of their power and propriety. Although honor rolls, gold-foil stars, and public recognition are totally external, they provide a pleasant association with a task that in itself may not be pleasant for a particular student. A student who does not like math may work diligently toward the goal of winning an honor for himself or for his team. Along the way, he may also develop a new level of skill and the internal motivation that comes from enhanced self-esteem and a sense of competence.

The power of the teacher's *expectations*—known as the Rosenthal effect—is sobering to consider. In one study, psychologists told eighteen elementary teachers that certain students, who had been randomly chosen, had extremely high IQs. Because of the teachers' higher expectations, the selected students showed a significant gain on an IQ test at the end of that year. Teachers should expect the best of their students academically and spiritually and should pray and work toward that end. With the Holy Spirit working in lives, the teacher has every reason to expect progress, even miracles.

Accountability teaches students to be responsible. Teachers should give their students projects with set standards of performance. Students need jobs to do, and they need to be motivated to do them properly.

Competition is a healthy motivator and may provide just the stimulus to cause a certain student to discover his potential. Teachers can carry competition too far and should take special care with one-on-one competition; but team competition can be especially effective. Spirit weeks, class competitions, review games, and drills provide excellent ways to teach cooperation, goal orientation, and responsibility.

The students' *homes* are an important but greatly overlooked resource. The parents usually care even more than the teacher about their children's progress. If a teacher establishes good lines of communication with parents early in the year, the parents can become the teacher's strongest supporters. Parents want to know not only the problem but also what they can do about it. The teacher will find that he has "assistant teachers" at home if he offers parents a kind but frank analysis of a child's problem and a plan to correct the problem.

Peer pressure is an especially strong motivator during adolescence, although it certainly is not limited to that time of life. The Christian school should constantly strive to create positive peer pressure: it should be "in" to study, to witness, to be separate from sin, and to achieve for the glory of God. The faculty and administration have the responsibility of setting spiritual as well as academic standards for those students who hold leadership positions. Usually the students most admired and emulated—the pacesetters—are the athletes and cheer-leaders. Therefore, they must especially have the right attitudes and actions, because they serve as role models for other students.

Additionally, the administration must be willing to "purge out the old leaven" of sin, because "a little leaven leaveneth the whole lump" (I Cor. 5:7, 6). This cleansing should not be a wanton, reactionary explosion but part of a careful, consistent program. A student and his parents should not be surprised by drastic measures; they should be aware of the school's efforts to correct specific problem areas prior to the administration of discipline. Sometimes students must be expelled or refused reenrollment on the basis of their bad attitudes and influence, even if they have not violated the "big" rules of the school.

Pressures, both positive and negative, can develop desired inward qualities, including the quality of internal motivation. In our stressful society, where even elementary school students are susceptible to ulcers, teachers should use the negative pressures with care. A wise use of positive and negative pressures will help accomplish the task of developing mature students.

Praise for Learning

The most important motivator is praise. Praise imparts love, warmth, direction, values, esteem—all the things that build up the inward motivation to do right because the *doer* is right. Proverbs extolls the power of positive words:

Heaviness in the heart of man maketh it stoop: but a good word maketh it glad. (Prov. 12:25)

A man hath joy by the answer of his mouth: and a word spoken in due season, how good is it! (Prov. 15:23)

Pleasant words are as an honeycomb, sweet to the soul, and health to the bones. (Prov. 16:24)

Young people hunger for sincere praise. They struggle, searching for an identity, and whatever the teacher praises will be repeated. The teacher who learns to praise has mastered the most powerful tool of interpersonal relationships and will help shape young people for time and eternity.

True Motivation

"Do all to the glory of God!" This is the true motivation, the ultimate goal of the Christian teacher; anything less leaves the Christian teacher on the merely behavioristic, mechanistic level of his humanist counterpart. There are many ways to motivate students—from sticker charts to the threat of expulsion—and most have their proper place and use. Christian schools ought to seek to develop in their students the inward desire to please God.

Although we may strive to be wise and skillful teachers, the Holy Spirit does the work in students' hearts. With all of our planning and working, we must also fervently pray and humbly depend upon God to do the work that counts. Only God can ultimately motivate from within (Phil. 2:13).

Ideas for Motivators

Love the Students
1. Show the students that you love them.
2. Take time for individual explanation to communicate both information and caring.
3. Be friendly and approachable. Talk to students about their needs and interests inside and outside the classroom. Pray with them.

Make Students Feel Important
1. Involve the students and encourage them to ask questions and offer input.
2. Encourage students to bring in materials that relate to the current lessons.
3. Welcome their questions with your words, face, and tone of voice.
4. Use small-group projects. To encourage interdependence, design them so that everyone must do his part.

Stimulate Interest in the Material
1. Use much visual stimulation: bulletin boards, bright colors, objects, good lighting, bright paint (elementary grades especially).
2. Have a table of things that the students may handle and try (elementary grades especially).
3. Establish a class library.
4. Bring in materials, specimens, and samples.
5. Use films, filmstrips, videos, and other audio-visual aids.
6. Be enthusiastic about the material.
7. Discuss your own related experiences.
8. Appeal to the students' curiosity. Use leading questions. Leave problems for students to resolve. Let these be written sometimes, so that it is not just the hand-raiser who gets involved.
9. Remember that novelty always gets (at least temporary) attention.

Make the Material Worthwhile
1. Begin and end in logical places.
2. Relate the material to Christian service or other specific goals.
3. Relate the material to the students' everyday world.
4. Relate the material to current events that your students ought to know.

Encourage Students to DO the Right Actions
1. Make it clear that they must do the work. Students should not be allowed to fail quietly.
2. Require students to maintain a minimum grade average (usually C- with no F's) to participate in extracurricular activities, such as sports or school plays.
3. Keep the students from quitting consciously or unconsciously. The student looks to you; when you give up, so does he.
4. Confront a student with a problem area; let him know by your face, tone, and words that you are not pleased; then encourage and smile.
5. Let the students know by your face, tone, and words that you are upset when improprieties occur.

6. Expect your students to achieve. Students tend to live up to their teacher's expectations, even when those expectations are not consciously expressed.
7. Enlist parents' help and keep them informed. They are usually more concerned about their child than you are. They will usually welcome your suggestions for something that they can do to help their child.

Praise the Students
1. Praise achievers, thereby motivating spectators to do better.
2. Praise publicly; criticize privately. Praise must be honest to be effective. Try as hard to catch them doing right as you do to catch them doing wrong.
3. Keep records of those you have praised or encouraged so that you do not leave anyone out.
4. Write comments on papers (e.g., "Way to go, Sue!" or "Much improved!").
5. Send encouraging/praising notes to the students.
6. Send notes to parents notifying them of their children's successes.
7. Encourage the students' attempts to meet your expectations.

Reward the Students
1. Have a "Good Work" board. Display improvement papers as well as A papers.
2. Use sticker charts—a sticker for each book read, practice sheet done, etc.
3. Make honor buttons.
4. Use hand stamps to honor achievement. This brings parental praise.
5. Give special privileges or treats for accomplishment.
6. Have a classroom honor roll if there is not an honor roll produced schoolwide. If there is a schoolwide honor roll, post a copy in your classroom.

Help Students Succeed
1. Provide opportunities for success. Call on students when you think they know the answer. Give them work that they can and will do. Match projects to people (especially science projects, reports, and art projects).
2. Make failure as rare as possible for each child.

3. Break goals into small tasks, each of which can be accomplished with ease. Then praise each accomplishment.
4. Take time to let students work problems through. When you ask a question, do not hastily answer it. Wait five or ten seconds. Call on two or three people. If an answer is partly correct, you or other students can build on that rather than call it wrong.
5. Help the students recognize their own successes.

Chapter 10
Teaching with Discipline

For whom the Lord loveth he chasteneth, and scourgeth every son whom he receiveth. . . . Now no chastening for the present seemeth to be joyous, but grievous: nevertheless afterward it yieldeth the peaceable fruit of righteousness unto them which are exercised thereby. (Heb. 12:6, 11)

Let every soul be subject unto the higher powers. For there is no power but of God: the powers that be are ordained of God. Whosoever therefore resisteth the power, resisteth the ordinance of God. (Rom. 13:1-2)

He that hath no rule over his own spirit is like a city that is broken down, and without walls. (Prov. 25:28)

One of the primary concerns expressed by education students even during their first year of college is discipline. These future teachers know that the academic and spiritual progress of the student is directly related to the right actions and attitudes that constitute a well-disciplined classroom.

Discipline constitutes more than mere punishment. The connotative associations of *punishment* are negative. Punishment involves administering the unpleasant consequences following poor behavior. *Discipline* implies a goal of making disciples. By balancing the positive and negative forces that not only prevent or respond to wrong actions and attitudes but also foster the desired habits, the effective Christian teacher will be an effective disciple-maker.

Chapter 10

Biblical Foundation

A procedure or a philosophy is not right simply because of the man or institution that promotes it. Nor is something right because it produces pragmatic results. To be truly Christian, a philosophy must adhere to a clear, Biblical pattern. Hebrews 12, which illustrates such a pattern, discusses God's discipline. The Christian educator can best handle a situation by thinking about it as God would think about it and by acting as God would act. "And ye have forgotten the exhortation which speaketh unto you as unto children, My son, despise not thou the chastening of the Lord, nor faint when thou art rebuked of him" (Heb. 12:5). The first principle to observe is that God does chasten. The Christian school teacher must be ready to realize that *he* must chasten as well. Although the teacher may be well-prepared and the students attentive, occasions for chastisement will still arise. "For whom the Lord loveth he chasteneth, and scourgeth every son whom he receiveth" (Heb. 12:6).

The mature and confident teacher has nothing to gain in a power struggle with children. Effective discipline proceeds from love. Loving students is the secret to having a successful ministry with young people. When students recognize this love, they will respond. An essential element of effective classroom discipline is the teacher's visible demonstration that he cares about the students, such as verbal encouragement and attendance at student activities. Love both motivates and empowers discipline.

> *If ye endure chastening, God dealeth with you as with sons; for what son is he whom the father chasteneth not? But if ye be without chastisement, whereof all are partakers, then are ye bastards, and not sons. Furthermore we have had fathers of our flesh which corrected us, and we gave them reverence: shall we not much rather be in subjection unto the Father of spirits, and live? (Heb. 12:7-9)*

These verses include a twofold assumption. First, all children receive chastisement; second, all fathers give it. Would that were true in our age! In an age when parents are inexperienced in discipline, when bribery replaces control, and when respect is an anachronism, children and teens often are unfamiliar with loving, consistent discipline. But they long for it, and they respond to it. "For they verily for a few days chastened us after their own pleasure; but he for our profit, that we might be partakers of his holiness" (Heb. 12:10).

Why does God chasten Christians? He chastens for their profit and for their well-being that they might grow. Why does the Christian school teacher discipline? The motive should be as worthy. Discipline should never come from frustration or a desire to strike back at a source of irritation. These motives might result in strong punishment, but they are counter-productive to discipline. Even in administering punishment, the teacher or administrator should remind the student that it is for the student's benefit. That assertion is a bit hard to assimilate while one is bent over the principal's desk, waiting for the imminent application of the "board of education to the seat of learning"; but a time will come when the student will comprehend the idea and highly regard the one who cared enough to discipline him with love. "Now no chastening for the present seemeth to be joyous, but grievous; nevertheless afterward it yieldeth the peaceable fruit of righteousness unto them which are exercised thereby" (Heb. 12:11).

Verse 11 is the key. Chastening is easy for neither the student nor the teacher. When the student has done wrong, he should know that the teacher is displeased. If the teacher does not treat the issue seriously, neither will the student. When the time for punishment comes, it must be consistent, fair, and significant.

Looking past His crucifixion to the great travail that would come on Israel, the Lord Jesus Christ said, "O Jerusalem, Jerusalem . . . how often would I have gathered thy children together, even as a hen gathereth her chickens under her wings, and ye would not" (Matt. 23:37). When the teacher or administrator feels the depth of compassion expressed in the phrase "O Jerusalem, Jerusalem," that teacher is beginning to discipline with the mind of Christ.

The negative aspect of disciplining is not enjoyable for anyone involved, but the result is worth the pain. The result of effective discipline is righteousness. Disciplining involves not only stopping the wrong actions but also fostering the right ones. Having a classroom of students who do right because it is right to do right and who consistently strive to please the Lord is worth any amount of effort and sacrifice to the Christian educator. The goal of Biblical, Christian discipline is not merely punishment; it is discipleship.

Procedures

Communication

Students cannot be expected to obey rules that they have never heard. In fact, there are times for clarifying and reviewing rules that they *have* heard. For instance, a rule pertaining to an evening basketball game might be presented at the beginning of the school year, but that rule should be reviewed prior to the first home game. There are many ways to promulgate the rules: handbooks, orientation meetings, chapels, and bulletin boards (especially in the elementary school). Every classroom should have a set of standard operating procedures, such as when pencil sharpening will be allowed. These rules are not profoundly spiritual, but they are part of an orderly, well-disciplined environment.

A vital part of communicating the rules is to communicate *Biblical* reasons for the rules. If a classroom procedural rule requires that students have two sharpened pencils and that there be no pencil sharpening during class, the teacher should give a reason for the rule. The principle "Let all things be done decently and in order" (I Cor. 14:40) is a good one. Another, recognizing the disruption and waste of time caused by a student's passing to the front of the class (inevitably jostling or flashing a big smile at friends on the way), is "Redeeming the time" (Eph. 5:16). Chapel is an excellent place for communicating the reasons for the standards, policies, and rules of the school. The teacher may want to take the same approach and have an in-room chapel sometimes.

If students are ever to internalize the godly standards of the school, they must understand the reasons for them. When students are never given reasons for the rules, they will accordingly forsake them all upon leaving the school. Success in Christian education, conforming students to the image of Christ, *demands* giving reasons for rules.

Enforcement, however, does not demand that the student agree with the administration's reasoning. The student may not believe that long hair on boys identifies one with the ungodly or is effeminate, but he still must obey the rule. Administrators are still accountable before God for what they allow, and often students require time to assimilate ideas that are foreign to them, no matter how clearly right. When they are given time to form their own convictions, students may not accept at once everything the school promulgates, but the convictions they form will be their own, and they will last. They must obey immediately; yet they must be given time to form their own convictions.

Control

After rules are communicated, the teacher's responsibility is to keep the classroom running smoothly and in accordance with those rules. Maintaining a comfortable environment is part of that responsibility. Problems are more likely to breed when the room is too hot or too cold or when the students cannot see the chalkboard clearly. Who sits by whom is part of the environmental consideration because some students are explosive combinations of independently harmless elements.

The teacher is the key to effective classroom control. The best method of discipline is a prepared teacher, and the teacher should keep the class moving at such a pace that students do not have idle time on their hands.

One of the teacher's principal responsibilities as disciplinarian is to be consistent. There are few weaknesses to which students react as negatively as inconsistent discipline. Whether the culprit is a cute little girl with freckles and pigtails, a basketball player, or the student who "never" gets into trouble, the application of the policies should be consistent. However, the first-time offender does not have to be dealt with the same way as the student who has a discipline record that reads like an FBI dossier. Nevertheless, the progression of punishment from first to second offense, etc., should be clearly and consistently applied so that the consistency is apparent to all.

What if the teacher has already been inconsistent? There is only one action that is right and honorable. In fact, there is only one action that will work: the teacher must admit to the class his inconsistency, declare that the rules will be consistently enforced, and then stick with his decision. Young people will always test boundaries, and the testing will be harder after the teacher has been inconsistent; but the teacher must hold firm for the students' sake and for his own.

Beginning in the junior high school, a system of classroom control should be instituted. Conduct grades and demerits are frequently used. In establishing and utilizing a system, everything depends upon having the "punishment fit the crime" so that the system is not laughed off as a joke. (*Effective Christian School Management,* James W. Deuink and Carl D. Herbster, published by Bob Jones University Press, devotes a chapter to establishing a control system.) In the elementary school, a demerit system is less necessary and is perhaps totally ineffective.

Working from the general to the specific is best in routine classroom control. If there is whispering in the back of the classroom, the teacher's first response might be a sudden silence and a long look toward the area of the offense. If it resumes, the teacher might make a general statement such as, "Remember, class, there should be no talking." Then, the more specific, "You, in the back of the classroom," or finally, "Tim. Tim. You, okay. Thank you." The teacher loves the student and does not want to make an example of him. (Consider Joseph, "a just man," and Mary, Matt. 1:19.) The teacher gives every chance he reasonably can before embarrassing a student or correcting him in front of a class.

Correction

Most routine offenses are handled in the ordinary course of classroom events and never need be thought of again. However, when a matter needs to be treated further, the school officials must be sure, first of all, that they have all the facts. School officials must never punish on the basis of another student's word. If a student comes to the teacher or administrator with an accusation, the school official should thank the student for his concern, direct him to *go to the offender,* and then promise to watch the situation or investigate, whichever is appropriate.

The intermediate step, going to the offender, is often omitted in Christian schools. This step marks the difference between tattling (informing an authority with a desire to get the offender into trouble) and dealing with a problem out of genuine concern for the offender and for the testimony of the Lord's school.

A student who knows that a peer is doing wrong should follow this procedure based upon Matthew 18:15-17.

1. Go to the offender and encourage him to correct his wrong behavior. This correction may involve making restitution and reporting himself to school authorities.
2. If the offender is not willing to correct his problem, the student should take another with him and approach the offender again.
3. Finally, if there is no response, the student should bring the issue to the attention of those who have the power to punish: the school authorities. Anything that ruins the testimony of the Lord's school and disgraces the name of Christ is an offense against all students in that school, and any student who is aware of the problem has a responsibility before the Lord to approach the offender.

If the offender says that he will repent and make the correction, the one who went to him should check up later to be sure that the offender has not just added a lie to his list of offenses.

This procedure is very difficult even for mature Christians to follow; and, admittedly, many young people will not be willing to follow it. Still, high schoolers are becoming adults, and they should be challenged to respond to problems Scripturally.

When the school officials have all the facts, they must administer the penalty fairly and consistently. It is wise to have predetermined penalties written down as part of the discipline system. When an offense is dealt with, records should be kept to determine objectively whether there is a problem with the student's frequently being in trouble. In most cases, the student who is a constant offender merits more severe treatment than the first-time offender. More serious cases, such as alcohol or tobacco use, or moral offenses, require the harshest penalty, probably expulsion, on the first occurrence.

Since the parents have the primary responsibility for disciplining their children, they should be notified when significant disciplinary actions are taken regarding their children.

The final step of any discipline procedure is to encourage the student to do right. The student should leave a discipline session feeling that the school cares, is on his side, and is cheering him on to do right.

The matter of discipline comes back to the foundation of Hebrews 12:6—chastisement proceeds from love. The teacher should care; and loving, consistent discipline is one of the most important ways that a teacher can demonstrate that care.

Practical Tips on Preventive Discipline

The effective teacher—
1. Learns the names of his pupils quickly.
2. Calls upon those pupils whose attention is wavering. This discourages daydreaming, interest in neighbors, and so forth.
3. Does not turn his back to the class and does not remain stationary.
4. Studies carefully the seating of the students. Certain students have a bad effect upon each other and form potentially explosive combinations.
5. Begins each class promptly and enthusiastically.
6. Is businesslike. Class time is for work, not play. However, businesslike classes should not be boring.
7. Is prepared with an interesting program of worthwhile material for each hour.
8. Watches his voice. It should be pleasing, but not soothing; varied, never a monotone.
9. Remembers that a sense of humor and a smile are very important tools in teaching.
10. Uses special occasions to show the students that he is vitally interested in them. He should go to the games and call or send cards when students are sick.

Practical Tips on Corrective Discipline

The effective teacher—
1. Stops the little thing, nipping the disciplinary problems in the bud.

2. Uses indirect warnings, then specific rebuke, to correct misbehavior.
3. Never humiliates in front of others, correcting students in private whenever possible.
4. Does not use sarcasm, scorn, or ridicule.
5. Does not make threats he cannot enforce and never uses the threat of withdrawing love or affection.
6. Is consistent in his discipline. He has no favorites.
7. Teaches that disobedience is primarily against God.
8. Allows the student to express his view of the problem. He helps him to evaluate his wrong behavior Biblically.
9. Always administers discipline with a heart of love, never in anger, since the goal of corrective discipline is to right the wrong behavior so that fellowship with God can be restored.
10. Always tries to handle his own problems, but calls for assistance when necessary.

Reprinted, by permission, from James W. Deuink and Carl D. Herbster, *Effective Christian School Management*, p. 147-48.